Blueprint
Creation, Disp

ISBN 9780990496359

TABLE OF CONTENTS

Preface

"Therefore, if anyone is in Christ, he is a new creation; old things have passed away; behold, all things have become new. (I Corinthians 5:17 NKJV)

There are millions of people who are the redeemed of the Lord, who are still trying to do things the way they learned them in the world. Yes, we live on this earth, but we are not of this earth; the Holy Scriptures declares that we are now citizens of the Kingdom of God.

"Now, therefore, you are no longer strangers and foreigners, but fellow citizens with the saints and members of the household of God..."
(Ephesians 2:19 NKJV)

As fellow citizens with the saints and members of the household of God, we fall completely under the rulership of God and of His laws. We are created in Elohim's image and His likeness; therefore, we are to operate on this earth the way He operates-completely by His Word. One of the biggest ways we set ourselves up for failure is by trying to be kingdom citizens living in the natural world and operating according to the world's ways of doing things. Although we live in this world, "we are not of this world" (John 17:16). We are flesh and blood like everyone on this earth but we live by and through the Spirit of the God, which the world does not know. We don't live by bread alone (food, toil, earthly wisdom) but we live by every Word (revelation) that proceeds from the mouth of our Father; His written Word and His spoken (revealed) Word.

As anointed kingdom entrepreneurs and sons and daughters of the Most High, we do have power. However, we must understand how that power operates on this earth and how to use that power. Our victory does not come from using the world's knowledge, wisdom or understanding to overcome and advance in this world's system; our victory comes from using the knowledge, wisdom and understanding that comes from God Himself. Yes, one can be a follower of Christ and work within the world's systems and obtain success and prosperity, but our Father's purpose, plan and blessing for our lives (and all the families of the earth) are only truly fulfilled when we operate on the earth using Godly principles and tactics to bring forth His will. It is only as we keep the Word of God continuously on our lips; "meditating in it day and night so that we are sure to obey it in everything we do (by receiving revelation from His throne), that we will truly be prosperous and have good success" *(Joshua 1:8)*

Section I
CREATION

Chapter One:
"And It was good..."

Anointed entrepreneurs are built to prosper. Anointed entrepreneurs are sons and daughters of the Most High, and we are created with the command to be fruitful, multiply, subdue the earth and have dominion over it.

Period.

The issue we run into with most of our kingdom businesses is that we form them in the earth before we ever create them in the Spirit, and this is not how our God operates. We are to operate like God on this earth; declaring the end from the beginning. Yet anointed entrepreneurs often put the cart before the horse because instead of declaring the end from the beginning, we *establish* the end before the beginning.

Let me explain.

In Genesis chapter one, we are given a clear description of how God created the heavens and the earth. All of creation was completed before Jehovah ever spoke a Word. Before our God formed the heavens and the earth, He created it all in his mind. That is why we are asked this question in the Scriptures;

> *"For who has stood in the counsel of the Lord, and has perceived and heard His Word?" (Jeremiah*

23:18 NKJV)

The word used here for counsel is a Hebrew word *Cowd*, which means; 'a session, a company of persons (in close deliberations), consultation, inward secret.' Before God spoke the heavens and the earth into existence, He had inward counsel within himself. Elohim created the heavens and the earth *in His mind (His imagination)* first.

Consider this; God the Father knew He was going to create man, so He set several plans in motion to meet man's spiritual and physical needs. God planned to create a being that He could breathe His own breath of life into; a being that would become a speaking spirit and a living soul. But what would a living soul require? The Father already knew that He would have to have a way to relay messages and get some things done so first He created angels; some angels to minster to Him and some to minister to the speaking spirits He would create. Since our Father created angels before He created the physical world, naturally the angels are spirits just like Him. However, man was to be a different type of creation; man was going to be a spirit housed in a physical being of substance. If God was going to create a spiritual being that had another substance or quality to his existence (physical flesh), He would need physical material to create this man from.

Elohim decided to create man out of earth, the substance of earth. Yet, before He could create man from the substance of earth, He had to create *earth*. We also know that man is more than earth, are we not? Our bodies are mostly water; so before our Father could create earth, He had to create water.

In the consideration of creating man as a physical being, there were other things that our Father had to set in place; how would a physical man with a body maintain the breath of life that God would breathe into him? There had to be a system that would allow the breath of God to be involuntarily maintained in the physical body over a period of time, correct? Our Father had to design man with automatic functions that the man would not have to force to make happen himself; lungs to push air through the body, a circulatory system to carry the air and respiratory system to breathe the air in and out of his body. Man would need blood to carry oxygen to the heart and brain and a heart to pump the blood through the body. Man would need veins to support the carrying of that blood and so on. When you think of all of the things that the human body does all on its own and continues to function on its own because, upheld by the Word of His power, there is no wonder David said in the Book of Psalm

> *"I will praise You, for I am fearfully and wonderfully made". (Psalm 139:14 NKJV)*

Once man was designed, how would the oxygen he needed to survive be produced? Man would need to get his oxygen from his environment; so God would create a firmament (atmosphere) that would hold vast amounts of the oxygen that man could breathe and move around in. God would create trees that would collect the carbon dioxide man would breathe out and turn it into the oxygen that man would breathe into his body. Then God filled the earth with trees and plants and animals, which would all have a part to play in sustaining the earth and providing for the man He created. God filled the waters with different kinds of fish and swimming things, all which would have a part to play in the ecosystem He would create. God filled the air with birds which would play their part in the ecosystem. God filled the outer firmament with the sun and the moon and stars which play a part in sustaining life on earth and separating seasons so things could grow on the earth. God designed all of this in His mind before He spoke the first word. That is why the Scripture, recording the creation of the heavens and the earth, tells us;

> *"The earth was without form, and void and darkness was on the face of the deep. And the Spirit of God was hovering over the face of the waters".*

(Genesis 1:2 *NKJV*)

(NOTE: Some will remark here that the heavens and the earth had already been created, which is why there is an earth because that is without form and void and that the waters are already there because the Spirit of God was hovering above them. However, that is not the focus of this discussion. We are currently investigating the process of the creation of the heavens and the earth. This is about the process; if we can understand the process, we can do the process.)

The the life-giving Spirit of God; the power that God operates by was now hovering over the face of the deep, waiting for the 'Word of God' to speak His Word (revealing the mind of God), that would create all the things God had imagined and counseled withing Himself as Elohim. Now was the time to create everything in existence that already existed in the mind of God. God had already created everything He was going to create; now He was about to form it by His Spirit through the *Spoken Word*.

This is also how we are to operate; we create it first through the revealed wisdom of God, then form it in the earth using the spoken Word of God, which prompts the Spirit of God to give it life. In the Scriptures, God says;

> *"For I know the thoughts I think toward you, says*
> *the Lord, thoughts of peace and not of evil, to give*
> *you a future and a hope." (Jeremiah 29:11 NKJV)*

Our heavenly Father is saying that He has already planned out your future and secured your hope. Your Father has done this already. Now it is a matter of you getting the wisdom of what He has prepared for you, and walking out what He has already designed by speaking what He has spoken; trusting what He has said and doing what He has said. That is how we obtain what God has created in His thoughts for us; receiving wisdom from Him about our lives and walking it out by faith.

The Spiritual Aspect

Consider the spiritual part of the creation. When God created man, He knew that even after He created the perfect environment for man and placed man in that environment and spent time walking with Man in the cool of the day, man would still disobey Him. God knew that his highest created angel, satan, was full of pride, jealousy and rebellion and that He would have to cast satan out of heaven. In His infinite wisdom, our Father knew that once satan inhabited the earth that He had created and given dominion over it to man, satan would use the wisdom given to him (by God) to deceive the man into disobeying the Creator. Then satan would be usurping the man's position of authority and dominion in and over the earth. It was satan promising the man that he could be like God and have the mind of God, that caused man to fall away in his imagination and then his reality. The deceptions was that man was already like God because man was created in God's likeness and image. The deception was that satan promised man that by obeying him rather than God, he would receive something he already had.

However, God was determined not to lose his creation and had already decided on a way to redeem man from the act of disobedience that would happen. God did all of this before He ever formed man, the heavens or the earth. God decided that after man had disobeyed and was subject to the wrath of a Holy God, he would delay fully collecting on that wrath until after He provided a way of redemption. The decision Elohim made was that He, Himself would redeem the man that He had created. God would send His Word into the earth; form His Word into a physical body just like man and His Word (which would be called Yeshua- Jesus) would take on the wrath required by His Holiness in the place of every man, so that the man He created could be reconciled to Him. All of these decisions were created in the mind of God before He ever formed one thing.

We are called to operate in the earth just as God did because we are made in His likeness and image.

So how does this translate to the entrepreneur, or to a son and daughter of God more specifically? How do we operate like God in entrepreneurship and in the earth? I have said previously that the issue with the sons and daughters of the Kingdom is that we don't operate like God does. God has anointed His Word, therefore if we want God's anointing as an entrepreneur, we must operate on the basis of His Word.

So, let's go through the creation as recorded in the book of Genesis and see how God formed the physical world, so we can see how we are to form our physical businesses.

Chapter Two:
The Process of Creation

"In the beginning, God created the heavens and the earth. The earth was without form, and void; and darkness was on the face of the deep. And the Spirit of God was hovering over the face of the waters. (Genesis 1:1 NKJV)

At this point, God has already decided in the counsel of His will (His council was the Father, The Word and the Spirit of God), what He was going to create and all the many facets of His creation both spiritually and physically. As anointed entrepreneurs, we are to operate the same way God operates. What is the business you are going to create? What are the facets of the business? What are the long-term goals? What will your business need to breathe and have life; a location, a computer system, a network of other companies or individuals? Who will your business touch over the first year, five years, twenty years and fifty years? Who is your customer or patron and where are they? How will your business grow? Will there be multiple locations? Will it be a franchise? Will it serve the local community, nation or the world throughout its lifetime?

As anointed entrepreneurs, we need to be able to see the creation before we form it. We must "declare the end from the beginning" so that we can go back to the beginning and breathe the life of the Spirit into it and declare that "it is very good." We need to know all about our creation; what keeps the heart pumping, what does it breathe, how does it eat and where its sustenance comes from. We need a detailed plan for our business before we ever start. Many entrepreneurs go off halfcocked; ready to start a business and put it out there before they ever take the time to truly create it. That is not how our Father operates and it should not be how we operate. When we don't create a thing before we form it, we are caught off-guard.

In 2020, the world went through what is deemed as a pandemic. Businesses were shut down and people were ordered to stay at home around the world. Many people and businesses were caught off-guard and as a result, thousands of small business and a number of large businesses closed their doors forever. Did man know that this would happen? Perhaps not. Did God know that this would happen? Absolutely. As kingdom entrepreneurs, should we have known that this would happen? Yes, we should have known something like this could and would happen. Even if we did not know the exact issue or the extent of the problem, if we as anointed entrepreneurs sought God from the beginning concerning our business, we would have received revelation from Him that we needed to put certain contingencies in our plan.

If we sought God from the beginning concerning the creation of our business, we would have definitely had a plan about what to do if business tapered off for some reason; even the world puts those type of contingencies in their business plans. In addition, if we are truly connected to God and acknowledging Him every single day, we would have heard something about making a change for our businesses because He will direct our path if we acknowledge Him in all of our ways. Furthermore, the scripture states,

> "Surely the Lord God does nothing, unless He reveals His secret to His servants the prophets". (Amos 3:7 NKJV)

Did the prophets prophesy in advance of the Pandemic of 2020? Perhaps; perhaps some did but few heard. Perhaps some received the Word, but were too afraid to say it because of fear that they were wrong or that they would be ridiculed. However, that does not matter in the end because of two reasons; (1) you are a friend of God and Jesus said He tells His friends what He is doing, (2) in the creation of the business (not the formation, the creation) we should have a contingency plan that covers a time when there is no income for whatever reason.

When you created your business, did you create a plan for operating without any sales for a period of time? Did you plan to forgo buying things and getting into heavy debt, so you could have some cash reserves in case you needed them? Does your business have a plan on how it will decrease its expenses in the event that not enough income was available to pay the business obligations? Did you create partnerships that would help you in the event of a market slow down? Have you created a way to adjust your business so that you could exist in another form during a recession; such as taking a physical product or service and adapting it to an online world?

This is creation the way God does it; He sees what is needed in the long run, not just what looks good in the beginning. God provides for the life of His creation in all aspects throughout the life of His creation. We are created in the image and likeness of our Father and therefore we should be operating in creation in the same manner the scripture shows that He operates. How are we to know what to prepare for from the start of our businesses if we don't know all of the possibilities of what could happen? We prepare by going to God. If you have been given a business idea that is from God and you are an anointed son and daughter of the kingdom of God, then you have the authority to approach His throne of Grace and receive wisdom and revelation straight from God. The Holy Spirit tells an anointed entrepreneur of things to come, if you are listening. The Sower is always sowing seed, but is it falling on good ground? If you acknowledge God in all of your ways, He will direct your paths. If you ask Father for your 'daily bread' daily, He will give you His Word straight from His mouth.

Some of you will say, "yeah, but how can we know all of the things that we need to think of, we are not God". I am glad we are talking about this point, because the next recoding of the creation answers this very question.

> 'Then God said, "Let there be light"; and there was light. And God saw the light, that it was good; and God divided the light from the darkness. God called the light Day, and the darkness He called Night. So, the evening and the morning were the first day". (Genesis 1:3-5 NKJV)

God created light and divided the light from darkness. God is light; God is the Word, God is revelation. Have you ever considered the fact that day and night does not depend on the sun and moon, but the revelation of light in darkness? 'God called the light Day and the darkness He called Night; and the evening and the morning were the first day.' Day and night have nothing to do with the sun and moon, because there was evening and morning before the sun and moon and stars were ever created. Get it; the light and the darkness, day and night came into existence before the sun, moon and stars were created (the sun, moon and stars were not created until Genesis verse 14).

So, what is this telling us? That the first thing created in a physical world was the revelation of God Himself. God is light and light is revealed in darkness; light was revealed while the object of creation was not yet fully formed. Light is the revelation of God in the physical existence, which dispels the darkness that was there. Everything in the spiritual realm knew God as light, but the earth was without form and void, and did not recognize God as light. Darkness was on the face of the deep. When God spoke His Word, "let there be light", God was revealing Himself to a creation that did not know Him as light, and then light existed- the revelation of a Holy, Almighty, and Omnipotent God was revealed in the darkness of the thing He had created in His mind and was now forming.

Anointed entrepreneur and sons and daughters of the kingdom of God operate the same manner as our Father operates. When we are creating our businesses, we are to get the light; the revelation of a Holy God in the thing we are going to form, which currently exists in darkness and is void. The light is revelation directly from the Word (logos and rhema) of God. What does this look like in action? Let's say I am going to start a mechanic business; I want to fix cars. During the creation process (before I ever form it in the earth), I need to seek God to get the light (day; information, wisdom, revelation) to overtake the darkness (night: the unknown, lack of sight). I must seek revelation from God our Father so that I will have the information, vision and wisdom I need to create my "world". I ask God for revelation so that He can reveal the deep things in Himself to me; so that the Spirit of God can search out the deep things of God and reveal them to me. I seek revelation from God about my mechanic business so that the mind of the Father can be revealed and impart wisdom to me. Finally, I seek God so that the things that belong to Jesus can be declared to me by the Holy Spirit of God. What things do we need declared to us, that belong to Jesus? Power, authority, wisdom, understanding, knowledge, favor, grace, mercy, goodness, love, kindness, revelation, direction...the light (incidentally, these things I just mentioned are also some of God's riches in Glory). Jesus told us that the Holy Spirit would give us all of these things and more;

> *"However, when He, the Spirit of Truth, has come, He*
> *will guide you into all truth; for He will not speak on*
> *His own authority, but whatever He heard He will speak:*
> *and He will tell you of things to come. He will glorify Me,*
> *for He will take of what is Mine and declare it to you. All*
> *things that the Father has are Mine. Therefore I said that*
> *He will take of Mind and declare it to you".*
> *(John 16:15 NKJV)*

What do we get from this 'Truth' that comes from the mouth of Jesus the Christ Himself? I understand Jesus to be saying that the Holy Spirit of God, the Spirit of Truth, will reveal to us everything we need to know about our business in advance; such as; deals, good and bad connections, recessions, pandemics, scams, opportunities and so on. The Spirit of Truth will set us on the path to creating our business so that the wisdom and knowledge of God Himself is intertwined into our business. How can you fail if you have the direct revelation (light) of God shining into your business before it is formed on the earth? How can you lose? How will you go out of business? If you did go out of business, wouldn't you know that beforehand, if you have gotten your revelation from God? Even if you didn't know your business was going out of business when you started, you would certainly see it well before it happened. You would not be blind-sided. How can I be so sure? I am sure because the Word says that the Holy Spirit will 'tell you of things to come.' However, just as evening and morning was the first day and it was the mark of every new day, we would need the constant revelation of God to know what was coming next. Just as God did not create everything in one day, but the revelation of His light (day and night) happened on a consistent basis in His creation every day, so must we continue to seek God daily so that the revelation of His light can come to us on a daily basis. That is how we pull spiritual things out of the heavenlies, speak them on earth and declare that "it is good". That is how the spiritual is manifested on the earth.

What does all of this look like when I am creating my mechanic business? I am going to start creating my business before I ever form the business. I am going to ask the questions needed; what does this business look like? What type of cars will I work on? Where do I find the people who has these types of cars? How many cars will my shop be able to work on at a time? How much will I charge? Will this be enough to sustain my business? What if it takes a while for me to get my customers in the door? These are just some of the questions I would ask my Father and record my answers on paper. Once I start asking the questions, God can reveal the answers; some of the answers will just come to us in our spirit, the rest of the answers we will have to do our due diligence to search out in the natural. Our Father tells us;

> *"The secret things belong to the LORD our God, but those things which are revealed belong to us and to our children forever, that we may do all the words of the Law" (Deuteronomy 29:29)*

and,

> *"It is the glory of God to conceal a matter, but the glory of kings is to search out a matter." (Proverbs 25:2)*

These verses take care of the spiritual and physical aspects of obtaining wisdom from God to form our businesses under the anointing of God. Our Father has all of the information we need to be successful as anointed entrepreneurs. God will give it all to us through His Spirit of Truth; but we must be diligent to seek Him beforehand; while we are in the creation stage, and not the formation stages of our business. If we wait until we have already formed our business, then we are asking God to bless our plans. However, if we seek God in the creation process, then we are asking Him to reveal to us the plans that He has already blessed- there is a huge difference between these two concepts.

The Spirit of Truth will reveal to us supernatural wisdom as well as give us knowledge and understanding for our vision; then we must continue to search out matters. The question now becomes; what information does God reveal and what information do we have to search out for ourselves? This is a great question and important to know. From our Father we seek out the things that are spiritual; the direction, what will come, the assignment, who we are sent to (because it is all for His will, not ours; He gives us the power to obtain wealth so that He can establish His covenant which He swore to our fathers- Deuteronomy 8:18). We need to be able to discern who He has sent in our lives that will help us in our assignment. The part that we seek in the natural is the natural part; how do we start an earthly business entity, how is marketing done, what tools do we need to have to do our business with excellence, and so on. We search out the natural things and depend on our Father for the spiritual things and for daily direction. That is how His "super" is put onto our "natural" which makes us a 'wonder' in the earth. This is why all nations will call us blessed; because while natural men are toiling to accomplish what they are trying to do, the favor of God is on our lives, and His revelation leads us to accomplish the same things supernaturally. We yield more fruit in less time when we operate on the earth the way God operates in the heavens.

Chapter Three:
The rest of creation and the business plan

Throughout the next five days of creation (the next five days of evening and night- God's revelation of Himself through what he was forming), we see the plan of God coming into fruition. We see God creating all of the elements that will sustain His ultimate goal, which is to form Man in His likeness and image. We see God creating systems for His creation to sustain itself, such as the ecosystem. We see God create processes that will sustain His creation such as photosynthesis, seasons, dew to water the plants, fruits bearing seed within itself and so on. All of these things God was creating to sustain His ultimate goal, the man that He was going to form and place on the earth to give dominion over all that He created.

In the same way we are to create our businesses. We create systems and processes that will sustain our ultimate creation; the formation of a physical business in a physical world. We do this through what is called a business plan.

Your business plan as an anointed entrepreneur is the Word- the Logos. The word "Logos" does mean "the spoken word", but it is much more than that. Logos is the intent behind the spoken word. What did you intend; what was in your mind before you spoke the word on the earth? We have discussed that God spoke all of these physical things into existence because He intended to form a physical man not only to be in His likeness and image, but also to operate in His likeness and image, and to have dominion over all of the things He created for man. That is why after each of God's formation of the thing He created, He said "It is good". "It" (the things He formed) was good because they were formed just as He intended and they operated and functioned in the way He intended them to function. All of God's formations came out the way God created them in His mind and they would support the functions that needed to happen; they would operate in the way He intended them to operate before He ever spoke the Word.

Therefore, when we are creating our business plan, we have to be intentional about what we are creating. This is why we need revelation straight from God Himself; so that we can be intentional with our creation, and that when we form it in the earth we can also say, "it is good". After we form our businesses in the earth, we need to be able to see that it is good so we can bless the business by saying, "It is very good; now be fruitful and multiply, subdue the earth and have dominion". This is what we want our business to do, correct? We were created to operate like God, so this should be exactly what happens.

Create your business plan. Create your business before you ever form it in the earth. Be intentional about what it is that you are creating so that when it is time to form it, you can speak the logos (the word and the intent behind it), and it can be formed the way you saw it. Remember the scripture; God formed all of the supporting systems of His intended creation (man), and everything was good. Once He finished creating everything that was needed to support the man He would create, then on the sixth day He created the man. With your business, the creation are the thoughts that you have about what it is that you want to form in the earth, and the business plan itself is the formation of the systems which will support your ultimate goal; the business itself. Your business plan should include sections on;

Executive Summary
Highlights

Once the business plan (the supporting systems) is written and declared to be "good", then you can move forward. You still don't form it yet. God created the man and woman on day six of the creation; on the sixth day He created them, He blessed them, He gave them their assignment and told them about all He had created for them. God spoke to them and blessed them on day six of the creation, but He still had not 'formed' them. You bless your creation before you form it. God created man and woman on day six, but He did not form man from the earth until Genesis Chapter 2:7. When God finally formed man, it was then that He breathed breath into man's nostrils. God breathed His very life into man. This is what we are going to do for our business. Once we finish the business plan, we are going to create our business through our words. We are going to name it (God called us man created after His image and likeness), we are going to bless it with words, we are going to give it an assignment of what it is created to do, and we are going to declare to our business the provisions that we have created for it from our business plan. Finally, we are going to pronounce it as very good. See how God operated in the sixth day;

> 'Then God said, "Let us make man in Our image, according to Our likeness; let them have dominion over the fish of the sea, over the birds of the air, and over the cattle, over all the earth and over every creeping thing that creeps on the earth." God created man in His own image: in the image of God He created him; male and female He created them. Then God blessed them and God said to them, "Be fruitful and multiply; fill the earth and subdue it; have dominion over the fish of the air, and over every living thing that moves on the earth." And God said, "See I have given you every herb that yields seed which is on the face of all the earth, and every tree whose fruit yields seed; to you it shall be for food. Also, to every beast of the earth, to every bird of the air, and to everything that creeps on the earth, in which there is life, I have given every green

herb for food"; and it was so. Then God saw everything
that He had made, and indeed it was very good. The
evening and the morning were the sixth day.
(Genesis 1:26-31 NKJV)

Male and female was created in day six, but not formed until after day seven. Just a side note; after Adam (man from the earth) was formed and in relationship with God, God said, "it is not good that man should be alone; I will make him a helper comparable to him" (Genesis 2:18 NKJV). God was not forming Eve because He saw that after He created man something was missing. God knew it was not good for man to be alone when He first consider His creation and before He created anything. God actually created Eve on day six when He created man, "He created male and female". God formed man before He formed Eve, but His wisdom was complete when He first created them. That is why we can be confident when we get our revelation from God that it is complete, and that we will have everything we need for the future.

Now we arrive at chapter two of Genesis; after everything has been thought out, after everything has been created and all of the supporting systems have been formed, after the blessing has been decreed by God over everything that He formed, then and only then does God turn His attention to the ultimate subject of His creation- man. God creates man before He forms him and speaks the blessing over man before He forms him. He shares with man all that He has created for him and give man dominion over all that is created before He forms man. Finally, God forms man from the substance that He created to sustain man- the earth.

This is how we create our business. We create it in our minds first by getting direct revelation or light from our Father. We form all of the systems that are put into place by creating a business plan that will provide for all of the eventualities that the ultimate creation (the business) will face. We bless each and every portion of the business plan when it is completed though our words; we bless the company description, the products and services, the market analysis, the strategy and implementation, the organization and management team the financial projections and the executive summary. We pronounce them as 'very good.'

We finish creating the business by searching out the business entity we are going to form; we search out where it will be placed, what it will look like, what is the vision and mission statement, what does the logo look like. Finally, after all of this work is done; after we have attended to the spiritual portion in which we received direct revelation from our God and we have searched out the natural information by doing our due diligence, after we have blessed the business and told it what we have put in place for it to run smoothly, and after we have told the business what it is to do, commanded it to have dominion and pronounce it as very good, then we form our business in the earth.

This is how we create a business in the likeness of our God; in this way the business will operate the way it was intended, God will get the glory and we have set ourselves up to prosper and have good success. We have an anointed business; anointed because it has been created in line with the Word of God.

Chapter Four:
The hands of the diligent

"The hand of the diligent will rule, but the lazy man
will be put to forced labor". (Proverbs 12:24 NKJV)

There is no doubt that one must work diligently in order to reap the blessings of the manifested Word of God, even though the manifestation would be based on the revealed Word of God.

"Do not be deceived, God is not mocked; for whatever
a man sows, that he will also reap. For he who sows to
his flesh will of the flesh reap corruption, but he who
sows to the Spirit will of the Spirit reap everlasting life."
(Galatians 6:7,8 NKJV)

I am aware that the above scripture is mostly used these days by leaders who are admonishing the body of Christ to sow seeds into their lives personally. However, there is more to this Scripture than that; there is a universal law of God in this Scripture.

"For he who sows to his flesh will of the flesh reap

corruption, but he who sows to the Spirit will of the
Spirit reap everlasting life." (Galatians 6:8 NKJV)

Where you are diligent to put your hands and efforts? What are you seeking after? If you are diligent to put your hands to work and toil after the things of the flesh, (meat, drink, money, clothing, shelter, cars and other natural things), you will reap theses things of the flesh, but they will lead to corruption. The things of the flesh lead to corruption because there is no eternal value. We see this every day; men and women working hard at their earthly education, jobs and aspirations in order to increase and move up the ladder of success. They buy things; beautiful houses and cars and jewelry and so on. They take time away from their families and away from the things that truly matter. When they are old and gray; on death's door, or their body can no longer support the daily functions of life because it has been broken down through a lifetime of abuse, that is when they realize that it was all vanity. I am not saying that one should not work hard and have nice things. I am saying what the scripture says; when you sow to the flesh, you will of the flesh reap corruption. We were not created to sow our time and energies to reap fleshly things. We were created to sow to the Spirit so that of the Spirit we can reap everlasting life; to know the one true God and Jesus Christ whom He sent. In knowing the Father and the Son, we will then receive revelation from them pertaining to who we are in Christ and what has been prepared for us in Christ. This way, all we have to do is serve our God, walk by faith and be diligent to His written and revealed Word to have more success than we can imagine.

> *"And this is eternal life, that they may know You,*
> *the only true God, and Jesus the Christ whom You*
> *have sent". (John 17:3 NKJV)*

The word used in the original Greek for "everlasting" and for "eternal" life are the same exact work, which means "perpetual". The point or focus of the eternal/everlasting life is; to "know the only true God and Jesus the Christ whom the only true God sent". When this scripture says "Know" God and "know" Jesus the Christ, the work used for "know is the Greek word, "ginosko", which is the form of a verb and means *'to have a working knowledge of, to perceive, to be resolved, can speak of because you understand'*.

Let's dig a little deeper; what does it mean to *"know, perceive and understand"* God and Jesus? It is important that we can understand what to know God and know Jesus means because this is the prayer Jesus prayed for you and I in John 17, that we; *"know, perceive and understand"* God and Jesus, because to do these things are eternal/everlasting life. Furthermore, the previous Scripture mentioned in Galatians 6:8 says, *"he who sows to the Spirit will of the Spirit reap everlasting/eternal life"*. Both of these scriptures are talking about the same kind of life, so what is the connection? Here is the connection; when we sow to the Spirit, meaning when we are diligent to work, labor and seek after Spiritual things, then we are in effect getting to know God and Jesus. When we have a personal knowledge of our God and Jesus; how they operate, who we are in them and what they have provided for us, we are getting to know them according to the Word. Jesus tells us;

> *"It is the Spirit who gives life; the flesh profits nothing. The words that I speak to you are spirit, and they are life". (John 6:63)*

Our God has created us to have dominion on and over this earth in all things (go back to the creation and the blessing God spoke over us through His Word before He ever formed us). Once we see that He has blessed us, called us "very good", told us to multiply and be fruitful, told us to subdue the earth and have dominion over the earth and everything He created in the earth, we will know Him and His intent behind the Word He spoke over us.

We see how He operated in creation and know that He created us in His image and likeness. We are to exercise our dominion in the earth to create our businesses the exact same way He did; by creating, then speaking His Word so that the Holy Spirit of God can form the Spoken Word in the earth. The Spirit of God is hovering over the face of the deep waiting for the Word of God to be spoken, so He can operate in Dunamis power and manifest the spoken Word (which is Spirit and it is life) in the physical realm. This is why we are to be diligent to sow to the Spirit and why when we sow to the Spirit, we reap everlasting/eternal life.

> *"He who has a slack hand becomes poor, but the*
> *hand of the diligent makes rich. He who gathers in*
> *summer is a wise son; he who sleeps in the harvest*
> *is a son who causes shame". (Proverbs 10:4-5 NKJV)*

It amazes me sometimes to look at all of these wicked people; people who spit on the Word of God yet are considered successful by the world's terms, while the children of the Kingdom are promised the blessing of Abraham and promised that wealth and riches will be in their house, yet do not receive the will of God in His Word. Why is this? There are several reasons, most of which come down to a lack of faith. Notice, I did not say belief, but I said faith. Belief is nice to have, but faith without works is dead. Faith must work a work to be true faith; faith is diligent to work. It is not by works that we receive the promises; it is by faith. However, if you do not put work to your faith, then your faith is dead. Even the atheist has faith that if they are diligent to work hard at a certain thing; if they learn a craft and connect with the right people, they can be extremely successful in what they have chosen to do. Jesus gave us a look into this when He spoke the parable of the "Unjust Steward" (John 16: 1-13). In the end, Jesus gave us a Word which said,

> *"So the master commended the unjust steward*
> *because he had dealt shrewdly. For the sons of this*
> *world are more shrewd in their generation than the*

sons of light". (John 16:8 NKJV)

Jesus goes on to say,

> *"And I say to you, make friends for yourselves by unrighteous mammon, that when you fail, they may receive you into an everlasting home. He who is faithful (diligent) in what is least is faithful also in much; and he who is unjust in what is least is unjust also in much. Therefore, if you have not been faithful in the unrighteous mammon, who will commit to your trust the true riches? And if you have not been faithful in what is another man's, who will give to you what is your own?" (John 16:9-12 NKJV)*

I can't tell you how many times growing up I have heard the phrase, *"your blessing is just around the corner"*. Nonsense, your blessing is with you. God has already blessed you; but faith without works is dead. You have to put diligent hands to work the work that He has given you. You have to put in the work; often times this is why the sons of this world are shrewder in their generation than the sons of the light; because the sons of this world will work diligently to receive the things of this world. The sons of this world will sow diligently to the flesh even though they will of the flesh reap corruption. The sons of the light are not willing to sow diligently to the things of God to get the revelation of what to do AND THEN be diligent in the forming of it on the earth. Faith comes by hearing the Word of God, but manifestation comes by diligently doing what you have heard. The Word that God speaks to you is the command and the power to accomplish the command is in the Word that was spoken to you, meaning; when God gives you a Word, the Word you are given is a seed. The power to produce the fruit of what was spoken by God is in the seed itself. The power to complete the task is in the Word that was spoken. However, if you are not diligent to plant that seed and water it; if you are not diligent to take action on the

Word that you have received from God, you will never see the fruit.

Let's view this in earthly terms. Let's say God tells you He has given you a company that will not only rival Amazon, but put Amazon out of business. That Word spoken to you sounds great when you hear it because you know that the owner of Amazon is the richest person in the world. So you figure that if God says He wants you to have a company that puts Amazon out of business, you will in turn become the richest person in the world. Well thought and well said.

Understand now that the power to create a company that puts Amazon out of business and become the richest person in the world, is in the Word God spoke, the moment He Spoke it. When God spoke that Word to you, He gave you His intent and His promise that it will happen. First, you have to receive that Word; believe that God said it, that He meant it and then you are to possess it by faith.

Possessing God's promise by faith is when it becomes real. To possess it by faith means you have to do something; you have to take that faith and put it into action. God has already told you he would give it to you, so the battle is already won because God goes before us and fights the battle for us, then He walks with us as we walk by faith into that victory.

But here is where the work of faith comes into play; do you know how to run a company? Do you know how to develop and grow an online store? Do you know how to put infrastructure in place to support buying and selling of other people's goods around the world? Do you know about warehousing and fulfillment? Probably not all that you need to know if you are truly going to put Amazon out of business. So now what? Do you wait for God to drop that information into your lap? Do you wait for someone to take you by the hand and say "hey, I have developed all of this for you, just come on in and take over"? Absolutely not! You have to work.

You have to get the information that you need to know to support this business. You will have to grow this business brick by brick. You have to ask God, "what have you put in place for me to do all of this"? God may say, "you need to get some education", which means now it is time to go to school, take some classes and get a mentor. Now it is time to start a small business and build it up from scratch. Now it is time to be diligent in working towards the calling that God just gave you. Now it is time for you to work the work by faith. Do something that moves you towards your goal; make some connections that can share information with you on how to do what God told you to do. Remember, if God gave you the Word, He has already straightened the path and put in place every person and thing that you will need, but you have to be diligent to get the information, create the connections with the people God has placed in your path to help you, and do the work.

Yes, there are some people in the world that the devil just gives his riches and fame to, but *most* of the people in the world have to work hard to obtain the things that others envy. If the sons of the kingdom of darkness have to work hard to obtain it, and they don't have the promises of and the Spirit of El Shaddai, why would you think that you don't have to be diligent in working out your soul's salvation with fear and trembling? You should be happy to put in the work; knowing that God has favored you so that you won't toil like the world. As you work, God will cause people, things, circumstance and situations to work in your favor to get you there so that He can be glorified in you.

Diligence. Have the faith to work the works of God because you know that He is faithful to bring to pass what He has spoken, and He has given you everything you need to accomplish what He has spoken. Our Father has given you His Word, His Spirit and the measure of faith; all you have to do is receive His Word, be diligent to work His Word and trust Him that He will bring to past what He has promised. We have the easy part, because God has done all of the toiling. We just need to be diligent to walking it out by faith.

Section B
DISPOSSESS TO POSSESS

Preface

One of the lessons that I learned early in my education was the lesson of displacement. The teacher told our class to go home and run a bathtub full of water. Mark the level of the water in the tub after we turned off the water, then get into the tub and take notice of the level of water in the tub after we got in. I noticed that the level of water had risen when I got into the tub. When we discussed this the next day, the teacher told us the water had risen in the tub after we got in because of the rule of 'displacement'. Our teacher explained to the class that our bodies were made of 'matter', and that two objects of matter could not occupy the same space at the same time. When we got into the tub, wherever our bodies were, water could not be, therefore the water in the tub rose to make up for the extra matter that was placed in the tub. This rule is very similar to our Father's intent in dispossession.

As anointed entrepreneurs, we are called to dispossess in order to possess. When we inhabit land that God has given to us, the current inhabitants must be moved out. We cannot be in our land and that land still be possessed by children of the kingdom of darkness.

> *"Now we, brethren, as Isaac was, are children of promise. But, as he who was born according to the flesh then persecuted him who was born according to the Spirit, even so it is now. Nevertheless, what does the Scripture say? 'Cast out the bondwoman and her son, for the son of the bondwoman shall not be heir with the son of the freewoman.' So then, brethren, we are not children of the bondwoman but of the free" (Galatians 4:28-31 NKJV)*

God has not changed. Our Father has not intended for His children of the kingdom of light to possess the land He has prepared for them along with the children of darkness We are to dispossess the land our Father has given us from the current inhabitants, and then possess it in their place. 'Friendship with the world is enmity with our God'; do not go in with the intent to take a little and leave a little. When God has called you and shown you what He has prepared for you, do not be afraid to go in that field with the mindset of possessing that entire industry; possess that entire kingdom in the place of the current occupants. This is what God's anointed entrepreneurs have been called to do.

Chapter Five
Modus Operandi

"And do not seek what you should eat or what you should drink, nor have an anxious mind. For all these things the nations of the world seek after, and your Father knows that you need these things. But seek the kingdom of God and all these things shall be added to you. Do not fear little flock, for it is your Father's good pleasure to give you the kingdom."
(Luke 12: 29-31 NKJV)

In order to operate in the kingdom of God we have to operate according to the light- the revelation of God. We are kingdom sons and daughters; we operate according to the rules of a different kingdom than we were physically born into. 'Beloved, now we are the sons of God' and we operate by the Word in God's kingdom. We should not look like the world and we should not operate like the world because although we are still in this world, we are not of this world. When we listen in on the prayer between Jesus and our Father right before Jesus goes to give His life as a ransom for us all, we learn the truth about our relationship to this physical world we live in;

> *"I do not pray that You should take them out of the world, but that You should keep them from the evil one. They are not of the world, just as I am not of the world." (John 17: 15, 16 NKJV)*

We are sons and daughters of the kingdom of God; entirely new creations according to the Word of God. When we were born of the Spirit into the kingdom of God, we became a supernatural creation; speaking spirits whose spirits are now alive to God through Christ. The Holy Scriptures are revelation from God on how we should think and operate in this world as citizens of a different kingdom; the kingdom of light as opposed to the kingdom of darkness. While the children of the kingdom of darkness are seeking after things to fulfill their natural appetite such as food, drink and clothing and while their minds are anxious for these things, we should be operating in another mindset all together. Our focus should be on seeking first the kingdom of God; His revelation, His will and His plan for our lives on this earth. When we make the kingdom of God our top priority, He has promised *'to give us every spiritual blessing in the heavenlies'* and to bless us with all of the natural things that we need to survive in a natural world. We see that during the creation He has already blessed us to "multiply and be fruitful, to subdue the earth and have dominion over it", therefore our job is to seek His daily revelation for what His will is (let evening become day everyday of our lives). By seeking our Father's daily revelation to us and doing what is revealed, we are promised that He will provide all of the things we need that pertain to life and to godliness.

Chapter Six
The Power is in the command

The reason that we need to seek daily revelation and receive a daily Word from our Father is because the power to live and to achieve His directive is in the Word (command) that God speaks to us. We see this clearly throughout the Scriptures; so we will use Jesus as our example.

Jesus came to show us the Father; He is the expressed image of the Father, meaning; Jesus was the image and likeness of the

Father living in the earth, just like we are created to be. When you saw the things that Jesus did and heard the things the Jesus said, you were looking at and hearing God the Father. Jesus always presented to us the thoughts and heart of the Father.

During the time Jesus physically walked on this earth, He was a man filled with the Spirit of God. Jesus was God in the flesh, but He was still born of a human woman; which means He was a man of flesh and blood just like us. Jesus' Spirit was divine, but His body was human. As a human man, Jesus believed that He had received a dictate, a command from God, and He believed God's Word to Him.

The amazing thing is, Jesus believed that He was God's Messiah before He ever received the Holy Spirit of God, and before He ever did one miracle. Jesus had faith that He had heard from the Father and was sent to save the world from their sins. In order to save the world, Jesus believed that He had to become a living sacrifice on behalf of the world to fulfill God's Word. Part of God's Word was that after Jesus gave Himself as a sacrificial lamb, taking on the sins of all of mankind, He would die and then rise from the dead and live again to take His place at the right hand of God Himself. I don't know about you, but to me this is a mighty tall order to have faith in as a human man. Sometimes I find the call on my life rather unbelievable, and I am not called to do anything near what Jesus was called to do.

Jesus believed that He would die, and then on His own, through the power of the Spirit of God which He had not even received yet, He would raise Himself up to live again. Do we understand the radicalness of this concept? Jesus had faith that after He suffered more than anyone had ever suffered for the sins of a world full of men and women that live before Him, with Him and for thousands of years after Him, that He would die, be buried and just get back up from being dead on His own. There would be no preacher there to pray the prayer of faith over Him, no priest to sprinkle anything on Him, no intercessory prayer team fasting and praying day and night for three days on His behalf. Jesus believed that after being dead for three days He would just get back up from being dead and be elevated to the throne room of heaven, right next to God Himself; that was the work that God had birthed Him to do. Now that is some kind of faith! Where did He get this kind of faith? Fortunately, Jesus tells us where He received His faith;

> *"Therefore, My Father loves Me because I lay down*
> *My life that I may take it up again. No one takes it*
> *from Me, but I lay it down of Myself. I have power*
> *to lay it down, and I have power to take it*
> *again. This command I have received from My*
> *Father." (John 10: 17,18 NKJV)*

What?! Jesus was not confident that He would rise up from the dead after three days because He had seen it done before, because in all of the recorded days that man lived on earth, this had not been done before. Nobody had died and just got back up three days later, on their own. Yet Jesus was confident that He would rise up from the dead after three days because He had received a revelation from God, a Word from God. Jesus had received a Word from God on the matter of God's will (command) for His life, and the power to complete the task was in the Word that God spoke to Him on the matter: and as far as Jesus was concerned, that was the end of the discussion.

A Word from God is not a suggestion; it is a command. Kings do not give suggestions, they give commands. When God speaks, He speaks a command; and inside that command is the power (authority and ability) to complete the command. Everything that you need to complete the work God has given to you is in the very Word that He spoke to you. Jesus knew that He had the power to do what had never been done before; give up His life as a sacrifice for the world, and after three days, stand back up alive because He received the Word (command) from God through revelation. God had spoken this Word (command) to Jesus through the written Word (the first five books of the old testament), and God had revealed this Word to Jesus through the spoken Word that Jesus receive when He sought God's will.

How do we know that God spoke this Word to Jesus in addition to what was written in the Scriptures for Jesus? We know that God revealed a rhema Word to Jesus about what He wanted Jesus to accomplish because that is the way God operates; He speaks His Word to His creation and to His people; we see and hear the proof of God speaking throughout the entirety of the old testament.

Since we know that Jesus is the expressed image of the Father and because we know that Jesus is our example of how an earthly man, filled with the Spirit of the living God operates on earth *("I am the Way, the Truth and the Light..."* John 14:6), we should operate the exact same way. We are to take all of the Holy Scripture, the written Word of God, and seek God daily for His revelation and His spoken Word to us.

Keep in mind that the spoken Word will always confirm and be confirmed by the written Word. Through the written Word and the spoken Word from our Father, we receive a personal Word (command) from God to us, and the power to complete the command of God to us will be present inside of the Word that is given to us.

Chapter Seven
Walking on water

We know that Jesus is the author and finisher of our faith. We also know that while Jesus was living on the earth, He was Emanuel; God in the flesh living among us. Let's take a look at how the power of God works in the Word (command) of God to us, using Jesus Christ as our focus.

In Matthew chapter 14, we see an example of how Jesus' Word is also a command because He is our God and our king. In Matthew chapter 14, there is a story that shows us how we are to act (and not act) when given a command from Jesus. In this book and chapter, Jesus has just finished preaching the gospel of the kingdom and healing many infirmed ones. Jesus blesses five loaves of bread and two fish, then proceeds to feed over five thousand people. After seeing Jesus do all of these healings and this uncommon miracle on this particular day, the disciples are given a simple command from Jesus; 'get into the boat and go before Him to the other side while He sent the multitudes away'. The disciples get into the boat and when Jesus sends the multitude away, He goes into the mountain to pray and receive more revelation from our Father.

In the fourth watch of the night, which is between 3am and 6am, Jesus comes to them walking on the water. Jesus, who is flesh and blood just like us, was walking on top of the water. The boat was in the middle of the sea, so Jesus was not walking on some land which was covered on the top by water; He was walking on the water itself. The disciples that are in the boat are recorded as being terrified and for good reason- who does that? What man just decides to cross a body of water by walking on it? If you were in a boat and saw what looked like a man walking on the water and coming towards you in the middle of a large body of water, what would you think it was? At least four of Jesus' disciples were fishermen by trade; they had been on the water for a lot of their lives, making their living off of the water as a trade. Had these fishermen seen something like that before; something that looked like a human being, walking on the water? I would suppose not, because if they had they would not have been terrified.

When the disciples become fearful seeing Jesus coming to them walking on the water, Jesus immediately says to them; *"Be of good cheer! It is I; do not be afraid."* God will always let you know that it is Him if you are afraid, because He has not given you the Spirit of fear, nor is He the author of fear. You never have to be afraid of circumstances or afraid of what you perceive, see, or think that you see. If it is God, He will let you know it is Him so you won't have to be afraid. If it is not God, you have power over it because *'greater is He that is in you than he that is in the world.'* You never have to fear.

Peter yells out to Jesus, *"if it is You, command me to come to You on the water."* This is crucial because Peter is asking for a command from Jesus; a Word from Jesus that has the power to accomplish the feat wrapped up inside that Word. Peter is asking for a command from Jesus to do what seems impossible for flesh and blood to do; to walk on water in the middle of the sea. Jesus' response is simple; He commands Peter to come to Him on the sea and walk on the water. What did Jesus say that had the power for Peter to do what was seemingly impossible? Jesus said, *"come"*. The reason I say "seemingly" impossible is because with man it is impossible, but with our God *all things are possible*. With God, anything you can think of is possible; and if you get a Word from Him, it is doable.

> *"For all the promises of God in Him are Yes, and in Him Amen, to the glory of God through us."*
> *(1 Corinthians 1:20)*

If you can find it in His Word, it is yours so He can establish His glory through you.

When Jesus told Peter to *"come"*, that was rhema; the spoken Word of God. The power to complete the command is in the Word of the command itself. That is why we are to speak the Word of God in earth; because the power of the thoughts of God which are recorded in the Scriptures, comes alive on earth when the Word (command) is spoken.

Jesus told Peter to *"come"*, and immediately, Peter had the supernatural power to walk on the water. The thing to note is that although Peter had the power to walk on the water because Jesus gave him the command, Peter would never have actually experienced walking on the water had he not; (1) gotten out of the boat, (2) stepped onto the water and (3) continued to move his legs and feet forward towards Jesus. You will not be able to walk on water or do the impossible in and with your business if you never actually do the physical actions the Word commands. The Word (command) of Jesus was *"come"* and Peter had to believe that the Word of Jesus was true and then activate his faith by taking action based on that Word (command) of Jesus. In this instance, Peter had to physically climb out of the boat he was in, put both feet on the water and take steps away from the boat and towards Jesus.

This is how we walk on water in our business and in our life.

Peter got out of the boat because Jesus spoke a Word to him (which had the power to do the impossible inside the word). Peter had faith in the One speaking the Word, which gave him faith in the Word itself. Note: Jesus could walk on the water because He had the Spirit of the living God in Him, but Peter walked on the water because he simply believed the Word that was spoken by the One who was the living Word. Remember, Peter at this point does not have the Spirit of God residing in him, Peter is simply a man following Jesus. At this point Peter is not yet endowed with the power of the Holy Spirit and he is walking on water just based on the command of Jesus to *"come"*.

How much more can we do as sons and daughter of the kingdom, having the Spirit of the living God in us and upon us? As sons and daughters of the kingdom of God, we have the written Word of God and we receive the spoken Word of God when we seek Him. Through the written and spoken Word, we have the power to complete every Word He gives us, because the power to complete it is in the His Word (command) when He gives it to us. Therefore, is it even possible for your business to fail when you trust and obey God's Word by faith? There is only one way that your business can and will fail; if you don't get out of the boat, put your feet on the water and walk towards Jesus, as the Word commands.

Chapter Eight
The Sin of Unbelief

Unbelief is perhaps one of the greatest sins. Understand; all sin is evil and cannot stand in the presence of a Holy God, but unbelief is a special kind of sin because it denies the person and work of God Himself, which leaves us in darkness. There are those who do not believe the Scriptures are the inspired Word of God. How then can they be saved? Salvation is by God's grace through faith, and faith comes by hearing, and hearing by the Word of God. If a person does not believe that the Holy Scriptures are the Word of the living God, they cannot develop faith; which means they cannot take advantage of salvation in Jesus' name which is by faith through the grace of our Holy God.

Unbelief presents many problems for the redeemed as well as the unsaved. Unbelief separates us from Jehovah, our God. Our relationship with God is by faith; the fact that we believe what God has said and who God is, comes through the measure of faith that God gives us;

> *"By faith Enoch was taken away so that he did not see death, "and he was not found, because God had taken him", for before he was taken, he had this testimony, that he pleased God. But without faith it is impossible to please Him, for he who comes to God must believe that He is and that He is a rewarder of those who diligently seek Him." (Hebrews 11:5,6 NKJV)*

Sin separates mankind from our Holy God and unbelief keeps mankind separated from God, because we have to believe in the One He sent in order to reconcile us to Himself. Unbelief in anything will keep us from enjoying that thing. For instance; if you don't believe that your spouse loves you, you will never be able to rest in their love or truly be at ease around them. Where there is no security.

Unbelief is magnified when it has to do with the things of God, because we were created in His image and likeness. No person can operate at their full capacity if they do not believe in the One who created them. Unbelief is an affront to our Father.

It does not matter whether you have accepted Jesus Christ as your Lord and Savior or not; you can still fall victim to the perils of unbelief. The redeemed of the Lord who say so, can also be found living in and with unbelief and completely miss the kingdom of heaven. Since God separates the unbelievers from the believers, for the sake of knowing the seriousness of unbelief, we will do the same.

Unbelievers

The designation 'unbelievers' is aptly named. These are people who have not believed in the salvation that is provided by the one true God, Jehovah, and Jesus Christ whom He sent. The title of 'unbelievers' is just that; a title or a designation. "Unbelievers" is a position or posture that man takes in relation to God. God is not a name; it is a position. Jehovah is God. Christ is not a name it is a position; a designation or title in relation to our God. Jesus is the Christ of our God.

Any person who does not believe that Jehovah is God and that Jesus (Yeshua) is Christ, is in sin and cannot please God because they don't believe that He is God. If you do not believe that Jehovah is God and that Jesus is His Christ, then you can have no connection to Him other than the grace that He gives to all of His creation because of His goodness.

As an entrepreneur, if you have no connection to God, then you have no access to wisdom; which is why you must toil to succeed. The only way to live in this world without a connection to Abba Father is by the rules of the god of this world, which means you are at his mercy (which he has none), and you will toil all the days of your life. There is no help in the world; there is only help in God because of Jesus. The Holy Scriptures declare;

> "But now I go away to Him who sent Me, and none of
> you asks Me, 'Where are you going?' But because I have
> said these things to you, sorrow has filled your heart.
> Nevertheless, I tell you the truth. It is to your advantage
> that I go away, for if I do not go away, the Helper will not
> come to you; but If I depart, I will send Him to you. And
> when He has come, He will convict the world of sin, and
> of righteousness, and of judgement: of sin, because they
> do not believe in Me; of righteousness, because I go to My

*Father and you see Me no more; of judgement because
the ruler of this world is judged." (John 16: 5-11 NKJV)*

This is the work of the Holy Spirit of our God, the Spirit of Truth. If
you do not believe in God, Jesus as Christ will not be revealed to
you. If you do not believe in Jesus, you cannot know God, and
Jesus will not send the Holy Spirit of Truth to you. If you do not
believe in the Holy Spirit or in His work, you are condemned in sin
because of unbelief. The Holy Spirit's presence on this earth will
convict the world of sin. Why of sin? Because the sinner does not
believe in Jesus as Christ, and the Holy Spirit comes to reveal
Jesus as Christ. You cannot begin to believe in God until you
believe in Jesus as His Christ. During His ministry on the earth,
Jesus has declared this truth,

*"I am the way, the truth and the life. No one comes to
the Father except through Me." (John 14:6 NKJV)*

First off, no one can know God until they know Jesus as the Christ
of God. Even those who claim to know God cannot know Him or
even be in His presence unless they believe in Jesus. The sin of
unbelief will keep us separated from knowing God and His Christ,
and there is no salvation in any other name. Therefore, the sin of
unbelief is deadly for the unbeliever, because in their unbelief,
they cannot have salvation which means they cannot have life. It
is one thing not to know the truth, but it is an altogether different
thing to reject the truth through unbelief.

When you run across someone who refuses to believe the truth;
someone who hears the truth but is determined not to believe
the truth, your heart should go out to them. They are in a
dangerous place. This is a sin that is difficult to overcome, the sin
of unbelief. Why is the sin of unbelief so difficult to overcome?
The sin of unbelief is difficult to overcome because to have
salvation itself, one must believe. It is impossible to please God or
to know Him though unbelief because in order to know Him and
please Him you must first believe that He exists. If you do not

believe that Jesus is the Son of God and that He died, was buried, rose from the dead, was seen after rising from the dead, ascended to Heaven and is now seated at the right hand of God the Father, then you do not believe the Gospel and you cannot be saved until you do. Unbelief will keep you separated from God in this physical life, and forever when this body goes back to the dust it came from.

Believers

Can a person be a believer and an unbeliever at the same time? Can a person believe that God is and not believe that He is a rewarder of those who diligently seek Him? Unfortunately, this is not only possible but quite often the case in the lives of many of God's people. It is because of unbelief that many of the redeemed do not walk in victory here on earth, and that many are not walking in the image and likeness of God. This means that there are many of God's people living far below their privileges.

A person can believe that Jesus is the Christ of God and believe in God and still not walk in the fulness of all that God has to offer. If a person believes in Jesus as savior, he will be saved and grafted into the family of God.

> *"if you confess with your mouth the Lord Jesus and believe in your heart that God has raised Him from the dead, you will be saved. For with the heart one believes unto righteousness, and with the mouth confession is made unto salvation." (Romans 10: 9,10 NKJV)*

The preceding Scripture is about salvation. However, there is more to living in the kingdom of heaven than just salvation. There is more to operating in the image and likeness of God than just salvation.

> *"But to as many as received Him, to them He gave the right (authority) to become children of God, to those who believe in His name; who were born, not*

> *of blood, nor of the will of the flesh, nor of the will*
> *of man, but of God". (John 1:12,13 NKJV)*

There is so much to unpack in the Scripture just quoted. The writer, John, is explaining the rights or authority (exousia) that is given to those who believe in Jesus as the Son of God and God's Christ. To those who received Jesus as the Christ of God; to those who believe in Jesus as the lamb of God that was sacrificed for their sins, so that they could come into relationship with a Holy God, to them Jesus gave the right to become sons of God.

> *"For you are all sons of God through faith in Christ*
> *Jesus. For as many of you as were baptized into*
> *Christ have put on Christ…. And if you are Christ's,*
> *then you are Abraham's seed and heirs according to*
> *the promise." (Galatians 3:26,27,29 NKJV)*

If you are saved according to the Word of God, you have become a son. However, there is more to sonship than just believing in salvation. Just because you are a 'son' does not mean you automatically receive all that God has for you. Consider this Scripture;

> *"Now I say that the heir, as long as he is a child,*
> *does not differ at all from a slave, though he is*
> *master of all, but is under guardians and stewards*
> *until the time appointed by the father.*
> *(Galatians 4:1,2 NKJV)*

So it is possible to receive Jesus to become a child of God, but never move into full sonship because of unbelief. Jesus gave authority for us to move into sonship through believing in Him and His Word.

> *"Then Jesus said to those Jews who believed Him, 'if*
> *you abide in My Word, you are My disciples indeed.*
> *And you shall know the truth, and the truth will make*

you free." (John 8:31,32 NKJV)

Jesus is talking to people who believed in Him. However, Jesus is saying that there is more than just the initial belief in Him to be obtained; there is an abiding in His Word, believing His Word so deeply that it lives in you and you live in it. If we have this level of connection to His Word, then we will know the Truth ("the Word of God is Truth), and the truth that we know will make us free; not set us free but make us free, meaning there is no other option but to be free. The Word of God will make us free from what? The Word of God will make us free from the curse; free from disobedience, poverty, lack, sickness, death, sin, fear, bondage, spiritual oppression- free from everything that is not His will for us.

There are many professing Christians who believe in Jesus and are not free because of unbelief. The Word (that we are to abide in) says that Jesus took all of our infirmities, healed all our diseases and by His stripes we are healed; yet there are many that are not walking in that truth. The Word says that God has provided all of our needs according to His riches in glory, yet there are many believers of Christ that do not seem to have all of their needs met. The Word says that He has given us everything that pertain to life and godliness, yet there are people who believe in Jesus that don't seem to have everything they need naturally and spiritually. The Word says we are the head and not the tail, above only and not beneath, the lenders and not the borrowers and that we are to owe no man nothing, but to love them. However, the children of God are not always the head but coming up behind, not above only but under the weight of tremendous oppression, not the lender but the borrower buried under the weight of debt. How do we account for this? Either the Word of God is a lie; a misrepresentation, or we are children and not yet moved into full sonship because of unbelief based on not abiding in His Word and His Word not abiding in us.

What does all of this have to do with being an anointed entrepreneur? A child in the kingdom of heaven will not have the full confidence nor the full backing of heaven on earth while they live in unbelief. If God says you are going to be so big that you will put Amazon out of business, you will never achieve that if you do not believe it (have faith in it). I don't care what it looks like or how impossible it seems. With man things are impossible, but with God all things are possible; but only if you have faith. Jesus said if we have faith as small as a mustard seed, we could move a mountain into the sea. However, if you don't believe that Word, you will be stopped by every mountain and mole hill you encounter. You will never achieve what you do not believe. Not in the natural and definitely not in the spiritual.

The Children of Israel Failed God and themselves.
God had delivered His people out of the bondage of Egypt by a strong hand. Through Moses, a man who believed God, God was able to deliver over a million people out of harsh slavery through wonders never before seen on earth. The children of Israel saw these wonders; they saw the judgements fall on the Egyptians which never touched them though they were living in the same land. The children of Israel walked on dry land at the bottom of the Red Sea while the waters of that sea were held up in a wall on both sides of them as they passed through. In addition to all of this, God promised to bring them into a land of their own; He promised to give them their own land which was overflowing with prosperity and provision. One would think that seeing what God did on their behalf to get them out of Egypt and keep them out of Egypt, there would be nothing that the children of Israel wouldn't believe God was able and willing to do for them. So it may be surprising to read where God brings them to the land that they are to possess, that they do not possess it because of unbelief.

> *"And the Lord spoke to Moses, saying, 'Send men to spy out the land of Canaan, which I am giving to the children of Israel; from each tribe of their fathers you shall send a man, everyone a leader among them."*

(Numbers 13:1,2 NKJV)

God delivered His people from a situation in which deliverance is impossible to mortals. God delivers the children of Israel by His wonders, sets them in front of the land that He has decided to give to them and He tells Moses it is okay to send representatives (spies) into the land first to have a look and see all that He has prepared just for them. The spies go in and return with their report;

> *"Then they told him and said, 'We went to the land where you sent us. It truly flows with milk and honey, and this is the fruit. Nevertheless, the people who dwell in the land are strong; their cities are fortified and very large, moreover we saw the descendants of Anak there. The Amalekites dwell in the land of the South; the Hittites, the Jebusites, and the Amorites dwell in the mountains; and the Canaanites dwell by the sea and along the banks of the Jordan.'"*
> *(Numbers 13:27-29 NKJV)*

> *"Then Caleb quieted the people before Moses, and said, 'Let us go up at once and take possession, for we are well able to overcome it'. But the men who had gone up with him said, 'We are not able to go up against the people, for they are stronger than we'. And they gave the children of Israel a bad report of the land which they had spied out, saying, 'The land through which we have gone as spies is a land that devours its inhabitants, and all the people which we saw in it are men of great stature. There we saw the giants (the descendants of Anak came from the giants); and we were like grasshoppers in their sight."*
> *(Numbers 13:30-33 NKJV)*

The Scripture goes on to say, that because of the report of ten of the twelve people that were sent to spy out the land, all of the children of Israel cried and wept that night because of unbelief.

The children of Israel did not believe that the same God that had just rained down hail from the sky, who had just sent locust and flies and darkness to cover the land of Egypt, who had struck the Egyptians cattle and first-born children (but left theirs intact), that this same God that parted the Red Seas could bring them into a prosperous land, in spite of what the current occupants looked like.

God had not only promised them something, He had also shown them His faithfulness in times just past. However, the children of Israel were not willing to believe that God would or could do what He said. Remember, God is a rewarder of those who diligently seek *and* believe Him. If you don't seek Him and/or if you don't believe Him to be a rewarder once you seek Him, then He will not be your rewarder. Only two of the spies, Joshua and Caleb, spoke up in faith saying;

> *"If the Lord delights in us, then He will bring us into this land and give it to us, a land which flows with milk and honey. Only do not rebel against the Lord, nor fear the people of the land, for they are our bread; their protection has departed from them, and the Lord is with us. Do not fear them.'"*
> *(Numbers 14:7-9 NKJV)*

Two of the twelve spies believed God. They knew that if God had brought them out of Egypt with a strong hand, and if He promised to give them this land, it didn't matter what the opposition looked like. God was with them and it would be to them just as God said it would. What was Caleb's and Joshua's reward from the people for speaking faith and belief in God?

> *"And all the congregation said to stone them with stones. Now the glory of the Lord appeared in the tabernacle of meeting before all the children of Israel. Then the Lord said to Moses, 'How long will these people reject Me? And how long will they not*

believe Me, with all the signs which I have
performed among them? I will strike them, and I
will make of you a nation greater and mightier than
they.'" (Numbers 14:10-12 NKJV)

When you believe God's Word to you concerning your business, not everyone you know or share your vision with will appreciate the beauty of it. You will experience people doubting you, discouraging you and actively trying to stop you. You may lose friends, loved ones and other relationships that you value. However, do not be discouraged; you continue to follow the Word God has given you and walk on that water. As for the people who walk out of your life because you are following the Word that God has given you, the Scripture tells us;

> *"So Jesus answered and said, 'Assuredly, I say to you,*
> *there is no one who has left house or brothers or sisters*
> *or father or mother or wife or children or lands, for My*
> *sake and the gospel's, who shall not receive a hundredfold*
> *now in this time- houses and brothers and sisters and*
> *mothers and children and lands, with persecutions- and in*
> *the age to come, eternal life. But many who are first will*
> *be last, and the last first." (Mark 10:29-31)*

God equated the children of Israel's unbelief in Him as rejection of Him. God's wrath wanted to stretch out against them because of their unbelief. Moses had to intercede with God in order for God not to strike them all dead. Do you see how serious it is not to believe God?

What has God told you about your business that you have not believed? If God gave you a business or an idea for a business and you are not walking forward in faith with what He has shown you, you are doing the same thing these children of Israel did. Let me tell you this right now, if you are not walking forward with what God gave you, then you are displeasing the King of Glory.

Thankfully, we live under the grace of God because of the blood of Jesus. The fact that Jesus is sitting at the right hand of the Father continuously making intercession for us in a greater way than Moses did for the children of Israel, should make us so very grateful and resolute to stop living in unbelief, get out of the boat, onto the water and walk towards Jesus.

The point is this; unbelief in the Word and promises of God is viewed by our Father as an outright rejection of Him. The children of Israel were judged for their blatant disrespect of God and His Word. All of the children of Israel that would not believe the Word of God died in that wilderness without walking into the plan, purpose and blessing of God. Their promised land full of prosperity and provision would not be inhabited by those who did not and do not believe the Word.

Only those who believed God lived to possess the promise of God. Well over a million people died in the wilderness "across the street" from the promise, because they would not believe God's Word to them. Rather, the children of Isarael believed a report from other human beings about what God could and could not do. Do you see how ridiculous this is? Well over a million people who had not actually seen the land for themselves, died in the wilderness because they believed what a few people told them about what they saw and God's ability to do what He said. What a shame.

How does that apply to you in your business? What has God told you He had for you? What has the true and living God promised to give you? Are you obtaining the promise through belief in His Word, or will you die in the wilderness because you will not believe? Have you lost access to the promises of God because you are listening to someone else tell you what your God can and cannot do? Your business will never be anointed and you will never possess the land that God has given you if you will not believe.

Chapter Nine
You have dwelt around this mountain long enough

I am finding that I love the Word of God more and more every day. There are so many beautiful Words, thoughts and sentiments in the Scripture that are written for and apply just to me. However, God has not forgotten you either; every beautiful word and promise in these same Holy Scriptures belong to you too. All of the Word is for all of the saints, and in a sense it is for the World too (even when it is not to the world), because it tells the story of a merciful and loving God, and the extent He was willing to go to in order to restore His precious creation.

I love that the Scriptures feels so personal when I read it. There are so many books, chapters and verses that I love to read and to hear the Lord reveal to me. I love all of the books in the Bible because God's Word is precious to me, but I love beyond measure the book of John; it really feels like a personal love letter from my Jesus to me. Two other books I love are the books of Deuteronomy and Joshua, because they feel very personal to me.

In the Book of Deuteronomy, we read one of the most caring and mindful Scriptures in the old Testament. It is hard for me to make this statement though, because on any given day and at any given moment, the focus of the previous statement can change. Here in the book of Deuteronomy is one of the most beautiful thoughts that our Father has expressed about His people and His desire for us all;

> *"The Lord our God spoke to us in Horeb saying: 'You have dwelt long enough at this mountain. Turn and take your journey, and go to the mountains of the Amorites, to all the neighboring places in the plain, in the mountains and in the lowland, in the South and on the seacoast, to the land of the Canaanites and to Lebanon, as far as the great river, the river Euphrates. See, I have set the land before you; go in and possess the land which the Lord swore to your fathers- to Abraham, Isaac and Jacob- to give to them and their descendants after them." (Deuteronomy 1:6-8 NKJV)*

If you do not hear the Spirit of God at this moment, let me share a prophetic Word for you right now.

"This day marks a new season for you"; God is telling you His intent for you right now, right this moment. The Spirit of God is saying to you right now that He is elevating you. You have been seeking His face and His kingdom; you desire to know His Word and His intent for you. You desire to do the work that He has assigned to you and you want to know how to do it. God is saying that this is the time that He is elevating you to walk into your destiny, to walk into what He has for you. "Do not be afraid and do not fear, for I am with you always", says the Lord Jehovah. "I have gone before you and I have cleared the way, I have fought the battles. I am walking with you so that you may maintain the victory in My name. You shall move on from this mountain, you shall speak to this mountain that has stood in your way and say to it, 'be thou removed and cast into the sea', and it shall move. Nothing shall stop you for completing the purpose I have set for you; nothing shall stop my Word from being established in your life. Only obey me and walk in faith. Walk forward and the waters of the sea shall part and you shall walk through on dry land. Walk forward and I shall straighten the crooked places, I will make your pathways straight. I will bring the resources and the people and the things that I have chosen to give to you that will glorify my Name. Only be of good cheer and be courageous, for the Lord your God is with you wherever you go."

What was happening in the first chapter in Deuteronomy is that the Children of Israel were being released by God to begin the process of possessing the land that He had promised to give to them. The children of Israel came to the edge of the promised land and decided they wanted to send spies into the land first, to get a natural report from men to validate what God had told them was available to them.

If you do not believe the Word of God to you concerning the command He has given you to possess the land (which is based on

His promise to you that He will give it to you), you too will cause yourself to be in a dangerous place. When you delay believing in and walking in the command that God has given you and decide that you need human eyes to look at the natural view of the promise, you will miss the promise of our Supernatural God. If you have been given a business and been told to possess the land in a particular industry, you will fail right away if you only look at it from a natural point of view, and discount the God that gave you the command. Your natural eyes will tell you that you cannot accomplish the task; there is a recession and no one will patronize you, or no one new to this industry can enter it and win because there is too much competition, or the last ten people who tried to do what you plan on doing failed miserably and lost everything they had. Your eyes and natural senses will lie to you and if you believe the lie you will not receive the promise. Your natural senses will have you walking around the same mountain until you die; physically and spiritually.

When you are disobedient to the Word God has spoken through stubbornness or unbelief, nothing will change in your life until either your body dies and departs from this earth or you die to the flesh and begin to walk with God; believing the Word He has spoken. *"For without faith it is impossible to please God" (Hebrews 11:6 NKJV)*. It is impossible to walk with God without faith *because, "how can two walk together unless they agree?"* (Amos 3:3)

Don't get me wrong, I am not saying that if you disbelieve God's Word to you when He first speaks it that He will turn away from you. Our God continuously speaks to us throughout the Scriptures (old and new testament), that He will never leave us, nor forsake us;

> *"Be strong and of good courage, do not fear, nor be afraid of them; for the Lord your God, He is the One that goes with you. He will not leave you nor forsake you." (Deuteronomy 31:6 NKJV)*

and,

> *"And the Lord, He is the One who goes before you, He will be with you. He will not leave you nor forsake you; do not fear nor be dismayed." (Deuteronomy 31:8 NKJV)*

and,

> *"And David said to his son Solomon, 'Be strong and of good courage, and do it; do not fear nor be dismayed, for the Lord God- my God- will be with you. He will not leave you nor forsake you, until you have finished all the work for the service of the house of the Lord."* *(1 Chronicles 28:20 NKJV)*

and

> *"Go therefore and make disciples of all the nations, baptizing them in the name of the Father, and of the Son and of the Holy Spirit, teaching them to observe all the things that I have commanded you; and lo, I am with you always, even to the end of the age." (Matthew 28:18-20 NKJV)*

and,

> *"Let your conduct be without covetousness; be content with such things as you have. For He Himself has said, 'I will never leave you nor forsake you.'" (Hebrews 13:5 NKJV)*

Our Father and our Lord have clearly stated that they will not leave us nor forsake us. However, make no mistake; there are consequences for disobedience and unbelief. There has to be consequences for disobedience and unbelief because, *"whom God loves He chastises"*.

We see in the history of the children of Israel, throughout the old testament, that even when God was displeased with them, He never utterly left them nor forsook them. Even though the children of Israel constantly tried God's patience through unbelief and through disobedience over and over, our Father was forever long-suffering and merciful with His people. Even when God swore that the children of Israel who rejected His word would not enter into His promised land because of their unbelief (by believing the word of ten human spies over the Word of the living God who had delivered them over and over), He was with them every day of those forty years in the wilderness until each of the rebelling ones died.

Our God is the same today as He was back then; even in our unbelief and disobedience He suffers long with us. When we don't believe His Word to us, God does not leave us nor discard us. Our Father is full of loving-kindness and tender-mercies every morning; He continues to encourage us to believe His Word in the midst of our unbelief, by His Spirit. Our Father sends up people to speak to us and prophesy to us and encourage us to believe Him and trust Him, in spite of our rebellion to His Word. Our Father still provides for us and covers us and protects us, in spite of our hardened hearts towards His Word. Our High Priest, Jesus, intercedes for us to the Father constantly and consistently; reminding our Father of the blood that was shed on our behalf, so that all the blessings of Abraham would come upon us. If Jesus and our heavenly Father are so diligent to keep Their Word to us even in our unbelief, how much more would they manifest Their glory upon us if we would believe the Word and obey?

How blessed would your business be if you sought God on every issue and then obeyed what He said, when He speaks it?

Chapter Ten
Learn the ways of the Lord

Here is where we get caught up and discouraged; we finally decide to believe God's Word, but we still don't know His ways. We don't know how God operates, so even when He puts the land before us and puts us in position to possess the land (that He has already gone before us and fought for us so that we could possess it), we don't know how to dispossess the enemy so we can possess the land.

We are created in His image and likeness; but if we don't know His ways, we can't operate in His ways and we remain out of position, which causes us to be defeated. If God has given you an assignment in business, but you don't understand how God operates through you to take land He has given to you, you will not be able to dispossess the enemy in order to possess the land He has given you. Your business will never drip of the anointing, which allows you to reach the heights that God has ordained for you to reach...if you go anywhere at all.

Before God brought the children of Israel into their land beyond the Jordan River, there were a series of things God did to prepare them. During their time in the wilderness God reminded them of why they were there- God reminded them of all that He had done for them by His mighty and outstretched hand. God reminded them of the deliverance that He had given them in Egypt through His wonders.

The same holds true for the business that God has declared to you. The Holy Spirit will bring to your remembrance the things that He has done for you in the past to bring you out and to give you victory, when victory was unattainable for you in the natural. Keep in mind that your business is only ordained by God if you seek Him first. Either God speaks a Word to you about the business He has given you, which is a ministry He has given to you, or you have a desire in your heart (that He placed there), and you brought it before the Lord and He gave you the desire of your heart.

> *"Therefore, my beloved, as you have always obeyed,*
> *not as in my presence only, but now much more*
> *in my absence, work out your own salvation with*
> *fear and trembling, for it is God who works in you*
> *both to will and to do for His Good pleasure."*
> *(Philippians 2:13 NKJV)*

and,

> *"Trust in the Lord, and do good; dwell in the land,*
> *and feed on His faithfulness. Delight yourself also*
> *in the Lord, and He shall give you the desires of*
> *your heart." (Psalm 37:3,4 NKJV)*

According to Scripture, if you have the desire in your heart, that means that it is God's desire for you. If you delight yourself in God concerning the desire that is in your heart, God has promised to give you that desire. Your business is therefore blessed of God; and when you submit it to Him, it is anointed by Him.

As God then called the children of Israel to move on towards the land that He would give them beyond the Jordan River, He brought them through the land that He had given to their brethren who heard the Word of God and obeyed it. The children of Israel would have to pass through the land that was once possessed by the same type of giants that they feared; the same type of giants which kept them out of their land, that their brethren did not fear. Their brethern, the descendants of Esau and of Lot, dispossessed the same type of giants so they could possess their land;

> *"And the Lord spoke to me saying, 'You have skirted*
> *this mountain long enough; turn northward. And*
> *command the people saying, you are about to pass*
> *through the territory of your brethren, the*
> *descendants of Esau, who live in Seir, and they will*

be afraid of you. Therefore watch yourselves
carefully. Do not meddle with them, for I will not
give you any of their land, not so much as one
footstep, because I have given Mount Seir to
Esau as a possession. You shall buy food from
them with money, that you may eat; and you shall
also buy water from them with money, that you
may drink. For the Lord your God has blessed you
in all the work of your hand. He knows your
trudging through this great wilderness. These
forty years the Lord your God has been with you;
you have lacked nothing."
(Deuteronomy 2:2-7 NKJV)

There are some important things to realize in these previous
verses. First, the Lord is about to move them into position again
to possess the land and receive the promise that He had given
them. However, this process begins by them going through land
that was already possessed by their brethren who had possessed
their promised land before them by faith. The land that their
brethren possessed had to first be dispossessed of the giants that
were living there, just like the giants the children of Israel refused
to fight against when God first spoke His Word to them.

In your business, the first thing that God will often do is show you
other anointed kingdom entrepreneurs that have obeyed God
when He first spoke. God will allow you to see others who have
dispossessed the enemy that was previously in power, and
possessed the land in their place. One reason God does this is so
you will see that He is able to bring you in and to keep you in.

Another place that God's entrepreneurs get caught is that when
they see others that God has place in their land, they want to
possess what their brothers have. Notice that God says,

"Therefore watch yourselves carefully. Do not
meddle with them, for I will not give you any of their

land, no not so much as one footstep, because I have
given Mount Seir to Esau as a possession. You shall
buy food from them with money, that you may eat;
and you shall also buy water from them with
money, that you may drink."
(Deuteronomy 2:4-6 NKJV)

It is not the will of God that you try to take over what He has clearly given to your brothers. Sometimes kingdom entrepreneurs don't want to believe what God has given them to possess; we want to possess what our brothers have been given. For example, if your brother or sister has written a book on "how to hear from God", why must you write a book on how to hear from God? If your brother or sister has started a tee-shirt printing business, why do you feel the need to open a tee-shirt printing business too? Why are you trying to hone in on what they are doing? Is it because God is blessing them in their business (land) that He has given to them?

Your business cannot be anointed if you are trying to do what your Father has not given you to do; it can be blessed but not anointed, there is a difference. You are blessed of God in all that you do if you do it in faith, but you are anointed when you flow in agreement with what you have been assigned to do. Blessed will get you a house, anointed will get you houses. Blessed will get you a business in an industry, anointed will make you the head of that industry and not the tail.

Do not try to move in on your brother or sisters' business or idea; purchase what you need from them (whether you are buying product from them or instruction from them) and keep it moving. God will bring you to your land, but He will not give you theirs.

Our Father is merciful and he wants us to be encouraged. He will show us people who are successful in what they do; not to make us jealous, but to encourage us.

> *"And we desire each one of you show the same*
> *diligence to the full assurance of hope until the end,*
> *that you do not become sluggish, but imitate those*
> *who through faith and patience inherit the promises."*
> *(Hebrews 6:11,12 NKJV)*

Look at what our Father did next for His people before He brought them into their land; He let them see others who had faced the same adversity and had overcome, because they believed God at His Word;

> *"And when we passed beyond our brethren, the*
> *descendants of Esau who dwell in Seir, away from the*
> *road of the plain, away from Elath and Ezion of Geber,*
> *we turned and passed by way of the Wilderness of*
> *Moab. Then the Lord said to me, 'Do not harass Moab,*
> *nor contend with them as a possession, because I have*
> *given Ar to the descendants of Lot as a possession.'*
> *(The Emim had dwelt there in times past, a people as*
> *great and numerous and tall as the Anakim. They*
> *were also regarded as giants like the Anakim, but*
> *the Moabites call them Emim. The Horites formerly*
> *dwelt in Seir, but the descendants of Esau*
> *dispossessed them and destroyed them from before*
> *them, and dwelt in their place, just as Israel did to the*
> *land of their possession which the Lord gave them."*
> *(Deuteronomy 2:8-12 NKJV)*

Before God gave the children of Israel their land, He again brought them through land that He had given to another. God brought them through the land He had given to Lot; land that was also possessed by the thing they feared- giants. Lot's land was full of giants; they were as great and as numerous and as tall as the Anakim that they children of Israel had refused to dispossess. However, God was showing them how He had been with Lot, so that Lot would possess the land.

When you are ready to create the business that God has anointed you to create, there will be people of the world already doing it, because there is nothing new under the sun. God may give you a new spin on an existing idea, but there will be someone in possession of that land when you get to it. God may give you an idea for a new type of board game that has not been created before, but there is already a board game industry. Your job is to believe God, create the board game and then be diligent to follow His Word. God will be the one to defeat the enemies before you; those in that industry that are not of God and trying to stop you from entering that industry. Your job is to do the work and dispossess the enemy, by moving forward in the Word you were given and then possessing in their place as they are defeated (or removed from the place they are in as you move in).

Chapter Eleven
The fight will come to you

So when does dispossession begin to take place so that possession can take place? When and how does one start possessing their land? Before a person can start possessing their land, all unbelief must be eradicated. We see the pattern of unbelief being eradicated so that one can possess their land in the Scriptures. God will begin the entire process with a direct Word to you;

> *"'Now rise and cross over the Valley of the Zered.'*
> *So we crossed over the Valley of the Zered. And the*
> *time we took to come from Kadesh Barnea until we*
> *crossed over the Valley of the Zered were thirty-*
> *eight years, until all the generation of the men of*
> *war was consumed from the midst of the camp, just*
> *as the Lord had sworn to them. For indeed the hand*
> *of the Lord was against them, to destroy them*
> *from the midst of the camp until they were*
> *consumed. So it was, when all the men of war had*
> *finally perished from among the people, that*
> *the Lord spoke to me saying, 'This day you are to*
> *cross over at Ar, the boundary of Moab. And*
> *when you come near the people of Ammon, do not*
> *harass them or meddle with them, for I will not give*
> *you any of the land of the people of Ammon*
> *as a possession, because I have given it to the*
> *descendants of Lot as a possession.'"*
> *(Deuteronomy 2:13-19 NKJV)*

It was because of the children of Israel's unbelief, that they missed out on the plan of God for their lives; to receive a land that was flowing with milk and honey (extreme provision). The children of Israel that did not believe God was able to do what He promised, did not inherit all that God had prepared for them. God's plan for the children of Israel was to give them a land that

He had prepared for them Himself; a land where they would dwell in big beautiful houses that they did not build, and enjoy the fruits of vineyards that they did not plant- a land where provision would be plentiful.

Even though two generations of people did not enter the land God had prepared for them, God was still good and merciful to them. The entire time that the unbelievers were in the wilderness, banned from entering into the land that God had prepared for them and decreed to perish in the wilderness, our Father still provided their basic necessities. The children of Israel were in the wilderness for four decades, but God provided for them so that not even the sandals on their feet wore out. Our Father gave them what they needed to survive in the wilderness, even though they were not able to receive the very best that God had for them.

The same holds true for us in our lives, our business aspirations and our dreams. Do you want God to provide what you need to survive, or do you want access to all that God has thought of concerning you? Unbelief will stop us from receiving God's best; the actual plan of God for our lives. God plans for us to be healed, but if we live in unbelief of this, we cannot receive that healing. God plans for us to be the lenders and not the borrowers, but if we are operating in unbelief, we will never come into the natural realization of this. God plans for us to owe no man anything but to love them, but if we stand in unbelief, we will stay under the weight of debt our entire lives. God plans for us to be fruitful, multiply, subdue the earth and have dominion over it. However, if we do not believe that God has created us in His image and likeness, we will not multiply even if things are added to us, nor will we be fruitful even though we have the branches- or ability- to produce fruit. If we stand in unbelief of the Word our Father spoke over us before we were ever formed ('Before I formed you in the womb, I knew you. Jeremiah 1:5 NKJV), we will never subdue the earth nor have dominion over it; we will never possess our land nor rule over the kingdoms, or systems, of the earth while we live this life.

In order for your business to be anointed, you must believe God. Our Father will still make sure you have a dwelling place, even though believing His Word to you would have given you the mansion He prepared for you. God will even let you have that business, even though His plan was for you to rule over that kingdom (industry).

Let's look at how possessing the land happens, because it all begins with believing the Word of God, and a fight. When the unbelief in the camp was destroyed, God spoke His Word again,

> "Rise, take your journey, and cross over the River Arnon. Look, I have given into your hand Sihon the Amorite, king of Heshbon, and his land. Begin to possess it, and engage him in battle. This day I will begin to put the dread and fear of you upon the nations under the whole heaven, who shall hear the report of you and shall tremble and be in anguish because of you."
> (Deuteronomy 2:24,25 NKJV)

My God! This is powerful if you can catch a hold of it. The Word of God had given them the command (remember, the power to achieve the command is in the command itself), and told them what would happen before it happened. They were not even entering their land yet and God had already set them up for success. Our Father was preparing them to enter the land. Sihon the Amorite, the king of Heshbon was a giant, just like the ones the children of Israel that perished in the wilderness was told to go against. God did not back down and give His people a smaller target, His intent was still to bring them into the land He had given them to possess from the beginning.

However, this portion of the possession was not the final possession; it was merely the land that God was giving them to put the fear of them on the nations under the whole heaven! Did you catch that...God was going to let their battle and possession with this first land show every other nation under the whole heaven that they were anointed people of God, on a mission of possessing land, and that their land was no longer safe!

> "This day I will begin to put the dread and fear of
> you upon the nations under the whole heaven,
> who shall hear the report of you..."
> (Deuteronomy 2:25 NKJV).

What day was God talking about when He said "this day"? God was talking about the day that they believed God enough to do what He told them. The surrounding nations were going to be in dread and fear just hearing about what God has done for, with and through His people! Remember the promise God gave to Joshua,

> "No man shall be able to stand before you all the
> days of your life; as I was with Moses, so I will be
> with you. I will not leave you nor forsake you. Be
> strong and of good courage..." (Joshua 1:5, 6)

In the case of your anointed business, the nations would be the various industries and businesses.

This is the Word God has given to you and to your anointed business. However, there is more in the previous Deuteronomy Scripture. God told them that He had given into their hand, Sihon the Amorite, the king of Heshbon, and his land. Here is the part to take heed of; *"begin to possess it, and engage him in battle."* God had given them the king and his land. God had already gone before them and fought the battle for them. God had just declared victory over the king and his land, although the children of Israel had not yet fought; they had only just now heard the Word of the Lord on what to do and what He had already done for them.

In your business, when God speaks the Word, it is already done. When He gives you the vision, He has already gone before you and won the battle. Your job is to walk out the physical part on the natural earth that coincides with His Word that was established in Heaven. You have already been given the land.

God tells the children of Israel, "begin to possess it, and engage in battle." This is important; beginning to possess the land was not the engaging in battle part. How did they begin to possess the land before they engaged in battle? The word "and" sitting between there indicates that this is actually two commands, both with the power to achieve the goal embedded inside the command itself. The Word to the children of Israel was; 'begin to possess it" (the land that they were just told was given to them) AND "engage him in battle". The "begin to possess it" portion is the spiritual portion. You have to have the victory in the spiritual realm before you can see the manifestation of it in the natural realm. Remember Jesus giving us the Keys to the Kingdom of Heaven and telling us;

> *"And I will give you the keys of the kingdom of*
> *heaven, and whatever you bind on earth will be*
> *bound in heaven, and whatever you loose on*
> *earth will be loosed in heaven"*
> *(Matthew 16:19 NKJV)*

Actually, the New King James Version does not do justice to this Scripture in its translation to English from the Greek. The exact translation from the Greek (from the Interlinear Greek to English translation) says,

> *"And I will give you the keys to the kingdom of heaven,*
> *and whatever you bind on earth shall be bound, having*
> *been bound in heaven, and whatever you loose on earth*
> *shall be loosed, having been loosed in heaven."*
> *(Matthew 16:19 Literal Translation)*

Remember in the proceeding verses, Simon Peter has just answered the Lord's question about who He is. Jesus responded by saying to him,

> "Blessed are you, Simon Bar-Jonah, for flesh and blood has not revealed this to you, but My Father who is in heaven. And I also say to you that you are Peter, and on this rock I will build My church and the gated of Hades shall not prevail against it." (Matthew 16:7 NKJV)

Jesus was telling Simon and all of the disciples that He was building His church on the direct revelation that comes from Our Father in heaven.

The indication is that before something can be bound or loosed on earth, it must first be bound and loosed in heaven. God speaks His Word in heaven, and it is established in the heavens. When God reveals His Word to us from heaven, it is already established. We can then speak that same Word on this earth and operate in the truth of that Word on earth, by binding and loosing the things connected to the Word that is revealed to us from heaven by our God.

If God has given you a business, He is not actually *just* giving you a business; He is giving you a king and a kingdom to dispossess. That tee-shirt company is not just a tee-shirt company; it is an entrance into the fashion industry. You are to destroy a king; a giant in the fashion industry by dispossessing his land and kingdom, and possess it in his place. There were many kings and kingdoms in the land that God was giving to the children of Israel; and they had to destroy them one by one. The first king and kingdom you come up against will not be the only one nor the last one, because God's intent is to give you all the land. That means that eventually you will come up against all the kings and take over all the kingdoms, in the Name of the Lord our God.

In the process of dispossessing the current king and possessing in his place, God will put the dread of you on every business in that industry and in all the nations under the heavens; to let them know that the kingdoms of this world are now becoming the kingdoms of our God. God is not merely interested in you simply having a piece of the pie; Jesus came to restore all things to God. Ultimately when Jesus returns to earth the restoration will be complete, but in the meanwhile we are to take back from the enemy what he has stolen from mankind; and the gates of hell will not prevail in stopping the anointed of God from doing just that.

If we go back to the verse in Deuteronomy 2:24 God said, "Begin to possess it", which means we must possess it in the spirit realm first. We must believe the Word of God when it is spoken and agree with it. Begin to possess it in your mind and spirit. Let your mind and spirit and mouth agree with what God says by speaking it on and into the earth. How will you know that your mind and spirit agree with what God says? You will know that your mind and spirit are in agreement with the Word of God because when you are in alignment with what God has revealed, it will come out of your mouth ("...for out of the abundance of the heart, the mouth speaks." Matthew 12:34 NKJV).

Once the Word of God starts coming out of your mouth on this earth, it will be established on earth because you are agreeing on earth with what God has said in heaven. When you agree with God on earth with what He has said in heaven, His Word is established on earth just as it is established in heaven. That is how we operate in the likeness and image of God. That is how things get done; that is how your business is anointed, and you see fruit like you have never seen. That is how the dread and fear of you comes upon all the nations under heaven.

After we begin to possess it, God says, "and engage him in battle". Now we must understand how the engagement part works. When God gives us His Word, we are to internalize it, then speak it and move forward by faith. Just like Peter, in order to walk on water, we have to get out of the boat, put our feet on the water and start taking steps towards Jesus.

When God told the children of Israel that He had given into their hand Sihon the king and his kingdom, the first part of that sentence is, *"Rise, take your journey, and cross over the River Arnon"*. Before you can take an industry over, you must first rise up and begin your journey. Let's say your industry is the fashion industry; how much do you know about the fashion industry? What do you know about different materials; how to import and export fabrics, how a business operates, where large scale manufacturing is done, how to identify distribution sources and so on? You don't just walk into the industry and say, "I am here, bow down". You will be setting yourself up for heartbreak.

God never just turns over the whole land to you that He has promised at once, He gives it to you little by little, piece by piece.

> *"I will send My fear before you, I will cause*
> *confusion among all the people to whom you*
> *come, and will make all your enemies turn their*
> *backs to you. And I will send hornets before you,*
> *which shall drive out the Hivite, the Canaanite,*
> *ant the Hittite from before you. I will not drive*
> *them out from before you in one year, lest the*
> *land become desolate and the beasts of the field*
> *become too numerous for you. Little by little I*
> *will drive them out from before you, until you*
> *have increased and you inherit the land."*
> *(Exodus 23:27-30 NKJV)*

Just as the children of Israel took their land piece by piece and battle by battle by defeating king after king, your dispossession and possession will work in the same way. Be diligent; the first thing is to rise up, cross over the river of revealed Word through action, and walk in the revelation.

Before we complete this section, I want you to notice one more thing;

> "But Sihon the king of Heshbon would not let us pass through, for the Lord your God hardened his spirit and made his heart obstinate, that He might deliver him into your hand, as it is this day. And the Lord said to me, 'See, I have begun to give Sihon and his land over to you. Begin to possess it, that you may inherit his land."
> (Deuteronomy 2:30,31 NKJV)

Isn't that funny? Well is it? God gave them the king and the land, but as they were crossing over to take their place, Sihon the king would not let them pass though. When you take that ordained business into this natural world, do you think you will face opposition? Do you mean to say that you have a dictate from God, and the world will not just let you in? Why do you think that is the case? Could it be because the world doesn't like you, even though you may be the best at what you do?

Actually, the world doesn't like you, but that is not always why you receive opposition. God Himself hardened the king's heart. Why would God do that? Remember the initial promise; that God would cause the dread and fear of you to be felt by all the nations under heaven. God prepares for the ultimate victory when He sends us out to possess the land that He has given us, not just the initial victory. God's intent was to give all of that land into their hands, so the king was made to hate them and war against them.

Here is a bit of revelation; you will know the land that God is sending you to overtake next, because *they* will come out to battle against *you*. You will not have to go looking for the next battle or for the land that God have prepared for you to possess; you will know the next land to possess because the battle will come to you. When you start receiving strong opposition, particularly from the people at the very top of that particular ladder, it is time to rejoice; God is showing you who's spirit He has hardened and who's heart was made obstinate...God is showing you who's land He is delivering into your hand next!

Chapter 12
The Battle Rages On

Some may think that after a battle is won, the land is gained. However, that is far from correct. As long as you live on this earth, the battle will rage on. There will never be a time when you are not in a battle. Even during the wars that have happened throughout the history of the earth, although there may have been days where there was no physical fighting, they were still at war. Even when the fighting seems to have paused for a day or so, the soldiers were still at war, and were expected to be ready for the next fight at a moment's notice. The enemy of your soul, of your faith and of the kingdom of God is not taking a day off; when you don't see him, he is just preparing for the next attack. You must stay prayed up; you must stay in your armor and stay battle ready. The Holy Spirit will show you things to come so you can even be preemptive. If you stay ready, then you won't have to get ready.

I want to make sure that this truth is drilled into your thoughts; when God gives you the command to take the land, He has already given you all of the land. When God gives you the product, He has given you the industry. As you believe His Word to you and take your business to the world, God gives you victory after victory. People will wonder how you did it; how were you able to establish a company in an industry that you had no formal knowledge or education in? How were you able to get the connection and flourish, when others could not hold it together?

How was your company able to increase during a pandemic when larger and more established companies than yours went under?

The answer is simple; you have the Word of the Lord God to lean on and the Spirit of the Lord God in you to produce fruit. Your job is to believe and walk it out by and in faith. God fights the battles and gives you the victory.

> *"You wrestle not against flesh and blood but against principalities, against powers, against ruler of the darkness of this age, against spiritual hosts of wickedness in the heavenly places."*
> *(Ephesians 6:12 NKJV)*

We are supposed to be standing against the wiles of the devil. That is why we take up the whole armor of God, because we are called to stand- not wallow on the ground wrestling. Jesus defeated the devil and made us more than conquerors. The Spirit of the Living God in us is greater than every demonic spirit and fallen angel in all of creation. We overcome by the blood of the Lamb and the word of our testimony. You are to stand; your business is to stand. The purposes of God for you is to stand and be established in this earth. You are the image and likeness of the Most High; the business that you have been given was given to you by God Himself, and birthed by the Holy Spirit. That is why no man can stand before you all the days of your life; who on earth or in the heavens can defy Almighty God?

After God gave the children of Israel the victory over king Sihon by His Word, and they walked out that victory through faith just as God had said, God proved to them that they did not need to have any fear because He had done just what He said He would do.

> *"And the Lord said to me, 'See, I have begun to give Sihon and his land over to you. Begin to possess it, that you may inherit his land.' Then Sihon and all his people came out against us to fight at Jahaz. And the*

Lord our God delivered him over to us; se we defeated
him, his sons, and all his people. We took all his cities
at that time, and we utterly destroyed the men,
women, and little ones of every city; we left none
remaining. We took only the livestock as plunder for
ourselves, with the spoils of the cities which we took.
And from Aroer, which is on the bank of the River
Arnon, and from the city that is in the ravine, as far
as Gilead, there was not one city too strong for us,
the Lord our God delivered all to us."
(Deuteronomy 2:31-37 NKJV)

How is that for victory; God gave them everything! So what are you afraid of? Are you afraid because you heard the giants of Amazon, Walmart and Target were already selling what you are poised to sell? Are you afraid because you want to start a tax business but H&R Block, Liberty Tax and Jackson Hewitt are already dwelling in the land? What are you afraid of; why are you not moving in faith, knowing that your God has already given the enemy into your hand, and has given you all of the land? Why are you stopping at a vision of one company when God wants to bless you with multiple companies? Why should you settle for owning a mortgage company when you can own the bank(s)?

We as sons and daughters of God think too small; when God created the earth, He didn't stop at creating the Garden of Eden or at creating the continent of Africa, He created the entire masses of land that we live in today. When God created the heavens, He didn't stop at creating the space where the clouds exist, He created enough room to fill another portion of the heavens with the sun, moon and billions of stars and enough space for them not to be crowded upon each other. So when you create on earth what God has spoken to you in heaven, why create just a small space for yourself; why not create something that has enough room for you to bless all the families of the earth? If one man can envision and create an online store that billions of people use constantly, why can't a blood bought, Holy Spirit filled believer in God like you do even greater?

Let's look at what happened after God gave the children of Israel the victory over king Sihon and they took possession of all of his land and cities; surely God was done with them and they could rest now. Surely God's plan of what He wanted for the children of Israel was fulfilled with that one land, which included a bunch of cities they could relax in.

> *"Then we turned and went up the road to Bashan, and Og king of Bashan came out against us, he and all his people, to battle at Edrei. And the Lord said to me, 'Do not fear him, for I have delivered him and all his people and his land into your hand; you shall do to him as you did to Sihon king of the Amorites, who dwelt at Heshbon." (Deuteronomy 3:1,2 NKJV)*

Notice the pattern; the next king came out against the people of God, they did not seek after him. The fact that Og and all of his people came after the children of Israel, allowed them to see who's land God had given to them next. Don't worry when the enemy of any industry or business comes out after you for no reason; seek God because it is very likely God is just showing you the next land that He has given to you.

> *"So the Lord our God also delivered into our hands Og king of Bashan, with all his people and we attacked him until he had no survivors remaining. And we took all his cities at that time; there was not a city which we did not take from them; sixty cities, all the region of Argob, the kingdom of Og in Bashan. All the cities were fortified with high walls, gates and bars, besides a great many rural towns. And we utterly destroyed them, and we did to Sihon king of Heshbon..."*
> *(Deuteronomy 3:3-6 NKJV)*

Let there be no mistake; the victory over Og and the people of Bashan was a great feat. Og himself was a giant and his people were giants. Let's qualify what I mean by Og being a giant.

> *"For only Og king of Bashan remained of the*
> *remnant of the giants. Indeed his bedstead was*
> *and iron bedstead. (is it not in Rabbah of the*
> *people of Ammon?) Nine cubits in its length and*
> *four cubits in its width, according to the standard*
> *cubit. (Deuteronomy 3:11 NKJV)*

Og's bed was made of iron to support his weight. The length of nine cubits long and four cubits wide, according to the standard measure of a cubit, means his bed was thirteen and a half feet long and six feet in width. To need a bed this size means you are a pretty big guy.

The amazing part is that they had not even scratched the surface of what God had for them. Most people would be satisfied with these two lands, but God had so much more for them. Most people would be satisfied if they could have a business that could pay their bills and let them go on a vacation once a year, but God wants to give you a legacy that will last throughout generations. God said that His will is to establish His covenant;

> *"Remember that it is the Lord your God who give*
> *you the power to get wealth, so that He may*
> *establish His covenant which He swore to our*
> *fathers.' (Deuteronomy 8:18)*

God's purpose does not stop with you having a business just so you can have a nice car and nice house and a trip to Spain. You can have those things, but this is about ministry; God's purpose and Word for you is much bigger than a few nice things to have. Cars and houses and nice clothes are the things that the world seeks after, but you are not like the world; you are a son and daughter of the kingdom of God, and God has purpose and plans that are bigger than just paying your bills to companies owned by heathens.

> *"Then I commanded you at that time saying: 'The Lord your God has given you this land to possess. All you men of valor shall cross over armed before your brethren, the children of Israel. But your wives, your little ones, and your livestock (I know that you have much livestock) shall stay in your cities which I have given you, until the Lord has given rest to your brethren as to you, and they also possess the land the Lord your God is giving them beyond the Jordan. Then each of you may return to his possession which I have given you.'"*
> *(Deuteronomy 3:18-20 NKJV)*

God is not just interested in giving you land to possess so you can kick back with your feet up saying, "I've made it." God's plan is for the *"kingdoms of this world to become the kingdoms of our Lord and His Christ". (Revelations 11:15 NKJV)* God is interested in showing all of the earth that He is God. Therefore, you cannot stop at one victory or even two victories with your business. Once God has given you your land, you must continue to battle until God gives all of His people their land. This is the will of God for your business; and to come short in this is to come short in the will and purposes of God. This is why God anoints you and your business; so that through you He can bring all of His people into their land and bless all the families of the earth.

This is the purpose of the Anointed Entrepreneur.

Chapter Thirteen:
The Tithe and the offering

We have come to an area where most people miss it. To think that bringing the tithe to God and giving an offering to God is not required in order to possess the land that God has given you is pure folly. Quite a number of people who claim to live in the kingdom of God actually do not, because they do not keep the rules of the kingdom.

When we become a child of God through acceptance of Jesus Christ as our Lord and Savior, we are translated from the kingdom of darkness into the kingdom of light. When we are born again, we are born with a new nature; we become a new creation and we live by a new set of laws- the law of the Spirit and of life. As a child of the kingdom of God, we come under the rulership and dominion of our God, Jehovah. We are now required to live a life pleasing to our God because we are born of Him.

The issue is; we must obey all of the laws or Word of God; we cannot pick and choose which Word we will obey and which Word we will not obey. Our Father, in His infinite wisdom, has established the tithe and offering long before we were born. Some think it was established with Abraham, but that would be incorrect; the concept of bringing the tithe and giving the offering to God was established in the days of Adam and Eve, just like the prophecy that God would send His Son to redeem mankind from the fall suffered though the disobedience of Adam. The tithe and the offering were not only established then, but because of one man's refusal to obey the Word of God in reference to the tithes and offering, the very first murder was committed on the earth. That is how rebellious man has been about giving the tithe and offerings to our Holy God, from the beginning of mankind.

> "...Now Abel was a keeper of sheep, but Cain was a tiller of the ground. And in the process of time it came to pass that Cain brought an offering of the fruit of the ground to the Lord. Abel also brought of the firstborn of his flock and of their fat. And the Lord respected Abel and his offering. And Cain was very angry, and his countenance fell. So the Lord said to Cain, 'Why are you angry? And why has your countenance fallen? If you do well, will you not be accepted? And if you do not well, sin lies at the door. And its desire is for you, but you should rule over it.' Now Cain talked with Abel his brother, and it came to past, when they were in the field that Cain rose up against Abel his brother and killed him." (Genesis 4:2-7 NKJV)

The first born of Abel's flock, meaning the first born of each that gave birth, is the first fruits and the first fruits are the required tithe that God commanded of man.

Let's go over what all is being shown in this passage. First off, the reason Cain's offering to God was not accepted by God is because Cain was disobedient in the offering that he gave to God. Both Cain and Abel knew what God required of them to bring before Him because one was acceptable and one was not. God told Cain, *"if you do well, will you not be accepted?"* The translation of this is, *"if you are obedient, will you not be accepted?"* If God is talking to Cain about obedience in this matter, then it is obvious that God also explained what He would have them do.

Both Cain and Abel also knew that blood had to be shed in order to cover for their sins; they had heard this from their Father and mother when they recounted the story of their disobedience to God. Cain and Abel were told of the Word that God spoke concerning the curse they were now under; the animal sacrifice that was needed and why He gave them a covering made from the hides of animals;

> "And for Adam and his wife, the Lord God made
> tunics of skin, and clothed them."
> (Genesis 3:21 NKJV)

When God gave them tunics of skin (tunics made from the flesh of animals) as a covering for them, God showed them how to give an offering to Him and how to give a sacrifice of the blood, for the temporary covering of sin. Adam and Even shared this with their children as well as continuing the process of doing it themselves.

How do we know that Adam and Eve continued to give an offering to God of what they received? We know this because the Scriptures tell us that *"in the process of time it came to pass that Cain brought an offering of the fruit of the ground to the Lord. Abel also brought the firstborn of his flock and of their fat."* Cain and Abel knew that they were to bring a tithe, an offering, and a sacrifice for sin to God; they learned it through watching their parents. As we know the nature of children and their questions, it is unreasonable to think that they watched their parents do all of these things before God for decades and never asked their parents what they were doing and why they were doing it. We also know that Cain and Abel spoke to God as well because God speaks to Cain directly after he kills his brother, and because Abel's blood cried out to God from the ground. Abel's blood (life) could not cry out to God for the injustice that was done to him by his brother, had Abel not been in a relationship with our Holy God.

Before we go any further, let us establish that the offering that Cain and Abel gave was not just an offering but included tithes. God has not and will not ever change. In Malachi chapter three, when God spoke about the subject, He called it "tithes and offerings"- the two were together and not separate. There is no reason to suspect that when God talked about this subject to His children before this chapter and verse, that the two were not explained together as well.

Abram's Proof
Before tithing was established during Moses' time, it was established with Abram. If God revealed the tithe and offering to Abram, there is no way we can believe that He has not told this same thing to His first creation, Adam and Eve. Remember, in the creation process, God had already planned out the entire scope of the physical and spiritual creation. He didn't just pop up one day with Abram and say, *"you know what, I think I want to institute tithes and an offering"*. God would have established this in His counsel when He established the fact that the Word would be made flesh, and redeem us all from our sin against Him.

In Genesis chapter 14, Abram gives tithes to Melchizedek, and from the story we can see that Abram had spoken with God about what to do once He met with the King of Salem;

> *"Then Melchizedek king of Salem brought out*
> *bread and wine; he was the priest of God Most*
> *High. And he blessed him and said; 'Blessed be*
> *Abram of God Most High, Possessor of heaven*
> *and earth; and blessed be God Most High,*
> *who has delivered your enemies into your hand.'*
> *And he gave him a tithe of all."*
> *(Genesis 14:18-20 NKJV)*

Let's take a look at all that has just transpired. Abram regularly talked with God. Abram had just found out that his nephew Lot, who was living in Sodom, was taken by some kings who had overcome another group of kings (one of which was the king of Sodom). When Abram found this out, he took his own warriors, chased after the kings who had taken Lot and defeated them. Abraham had a limited number of soldiers and he was about to chase after four kings and their armies. Since we know that Abram regularly talked with God, we know that before he went after these kings, He brought it before God and God assured him of the victory and told Abram exactly what to do.

After Abram defeats all four of these kings and their warriors, Abram took all of the spoils of that battle with these kings and brought them back with him. On his journey back, Abram stopped off to see the priest Melchizedek, and present a tithe to the Lord God Most High. We know that Abram had spoken to God before the trip out to fight the kings and that God told him He would give him the victory, along with the directions to tithe and to give the king of Sodom and the other kings back all of their possessions Abram had taken in the battle, because of the following verses;

> "But Abram said to the king of Sodom, 'I have raised
> my hand to the Lord, God Most High, the
> Possessor of heaven and earth, that I will take
> nothing, from a thread to a sandal strap, and that I
> will not take anything that is yours, lest you should
> say, "I have made Abram rich"- except only what the
> young men have eaten, and the portion of the men
> who went with me: Aner, Eshcol, and Mamre; let
> them take their portion.'" (Genesis 14:22-24 NKJV)

Before Abram went to fight to get Lot back, this Scripture shows us that he went to God to get permission and to ensure his victory. God told Abram that He would give him victory in this battle and God told Abram what to do after the battle pertaining to giving a tithe and giving the kings back their property.

How do we know that Abram had that conversation and that God instructed him to do these things? When Abram returns, the first thing he does is give tithes. When Abram has the conversation with the king of Sodom, he explains his action as him having raised his hand to the Lord, God Most High that he would do certain things when he returned. If Abram's action to give the kings back everything that were theirs and keep nothing, then it follows that his response to God was also to give the tithe that God required of him in response to the victory God gave Abram in defeating kings with his three hundred and eighteen soldiers (Note: Abram defeated four kings with three hundred eighteen soldiers, where the five kings that originally went up against these same kings had failed. That is obviously the favor of God).

What was Abram's reward for keeping the Word of the Lord who had promised him victory? What was the reward for Abram giving the tithe of his spoils and obeying God in giving the kings back their possessions?

> *"After these things the Word of the Lord came to Abram in a vision, saying, 'Do not be afraid, Abram. I am your shield, your exceedingly great reward.'" (Genesis 15:1 NKJV)*

The result to Abram's obedience in the tithe (and offering because the two go together), was God sending His Word to Abram. Abram obeyed God and because of his obedience he didn't even have to seek out God, God sent His Word to Abram. Not only did Abram receive the Word that God Himself would be his shield and his exceedingly great reward, but God stayed to hold a conversation with Abram in which the outcome was a promise to grant what Abram most desired on this earth (besides God); a son of his own.

This is what obedience to all of the Word of God, including the tithe and offering, will do for you; give you an audience before

God Himself and the unmatched blessing straight from the mouth of God. In addition, God tells us what else the tithe and offering will do for us;

> *"Bring all the tithes into the storehouse, that there may be food in My house, and try Me now in this," says the Lord of hosts, "If I will not open the windows of heaven and pour out for you such blessing that there will not be room enough to receive it. And I will rebuke the devourer for your sakes so that he will not destroy the fruit of your ground, nor shall the vine fail to bear fruit for you in the field," says the Lord of hosts; "and all nations will call you blessed, for you will be a delightful land," says the Lord of Hosts." (Malachi 3:10-12 NKJV)*

Jacob's Proof

After the vision that Jacob received in Genesis 28; after God visited him and gave him a promise that he had heard from his father, pertaining to his grandfather Abraham and to his father Isaac, Jacob speaks many things to the Lord as an oath. One of the final things that Jacob says is;

> *"And this stone which I have set as a pillar shall be God's house, and of all that You give me I will surely give a tenth to You." (Genesis 28:22 NKJV)*

Just before Jacob spoke these words, God gave him a wonderful Word on who He was and what He would do for Jacob. Jacob promises to take this Word, believe it and even operate in the same way that his grandfather and father had acted towards the Lord in tithes and offering. Abraham was a tither and he passed that on to his son Isaac. Isaac was a tither and tried to pass that on to Jacob, but initially, Jacob was not living in that truth for a number of years. However, when Jacob has a personal encounter with the Lord God, who promised to do these wonderful things for him, Jacob now gives an oath to do all that his grandfather had done and his father had done concerning the tithes and offering.

Have you had an encounter with the Lord, God Most High? Has God blessed you? If God has blessed you and provided sustenance for you, then why would you not do what His people have done since the days of Adam and Eve concerning the tithe and the offering? If you truly believe that God has granted you favor to start a business and He has given you the power to get wealth, then it is your duty to be obedient to all of the Word.

God has spoken what he would do for the person who brings the tithe and offering to Him in Malachi 3:10-12, and His Word is forever established in the heavens. Furthermore, God declares that He watches over His Word that He has spoken, to perform it. God has shown us throughout the Scripture that He is with the son and daughter that obeys all of His Word. If you will commit to bring the tithes and offerings to God, I can say to you by the Spirit of the living God that *"He will be your shield and your exceedingly great reward."*

You will never have to fear about anything again and you will have all of the provision you need, if you will trust in the Word of the Lord your God;

> *"Honor the Lord with your possessions, and with*
> *the first fruits of all your increase; so your barns will*
> *be filled with plenty, and your vats with new wine."*
> *(Proverbs 3:9,10 NKJV)*

This is the tithe, the offering and the promise. Who will you believe; God or your natural senses and inclinations?

Chapter Fourteen
Reaching the other side

The goal of the Anointed Entrepreneur is to 'reach the other side'. We are given a Word from our Holy God that has within it the power to complete the task. God has gone before us and fought the battles that will come to us; the battles come as a result of God's Word to us because we are doing the work that is required to advance His kingdom.

The enemy of our faith and of our God does not want to see the plans and purposes of God advanced. Every piece of land we take for our God not only lessens the control the devil has over the earth and people in it, but it also shortens his time on this earth. Our adversary, the devil, knows that God's Work will be completed because he is already defeated. Jesus defeated satan already and gave us the authority in His Name to not only keep what was won, but to advance the kingdom of God under the direction of the Holy Spirit.

Your anointed business is your ministry; it is through this that God wants to bless all the nations of the earth. It is through your anointed business that God wants to let all of the earth know that He is God and there is no God besides Him. God will be glorified and He has glorified you so that you can carry the glory of God throughout the earth; lifting up the Name of Jesus so that the Father may be glorified in Him.

When God gives you the command, the goal is to reach the other side. The other side in this chapter is defined as "completing the word that was given to you'. Once you complete the Word that is given to you, once you reach the other side, you will be given the next Word. We walk by faith, not by knowing. We walk by faith, not by sight. We go from glory to glory, meaning that when we complete the present assignment that our Holy God has given us, it brings Him glory and we go on to complete the next Word of God and go on to glory again. God is glorified in us; we are the representatives of the glory of God on this earth. We are ambassadors of Christ. Through us obeying God, the Holy Spirit can do His work and God is both seen and glorified. This is what it means to glorify God; "to complete the work that He has given us", every command, every Word, every work.

The disciples
We read an interesting story in the Gospel according to Luke. One day, after Jesus had been teaching the gospel of the kingdom with parables and healing the people, He gave the disciples a Word or a command of what His intentions were;

> "Now it happened, on a certain day, that He got into
> a boat with His disciples. And He said to them, 'Let us
> cross to the other side of the lake.' And they launched
> out. But as they sailed, He fell asleep. And a windstorm
> came down on the lake, and they were filling with water,
> and were in jeopardy. And they came to Him and awoke
> Him saying, 'Master, Master, we are perishing'! Then He
> arose and rebuked the wind and the raging of the water.

And they ceased and there was a calm. But He said to them, 'Where is your faith?" (Luke 8:22-25 NKJV)

Let's unpack a lesson from this story. Jesus, whom the disciples had seen work miracle after miracle, whom they were following as the Christ of God, is in the beginning times of His ministry on earth. Jesus tells them, *"let us cross to the other side".* Jesus then gets into the boat with His disciples. Jesus is with them as they launch out to complete the Word that He had spoken to them.

Note: In your business and in your life, when you hear the voice of the Lord telling you what to do, to *"cross over to the other side"* of the command that He is giving you, He launches out with you. Our God and our Jesus has promised never to leave us nor forsake us.

The disciples followed His command from the start; they got into the boat and launched off with the intent to go to the other side. During the trip (after they launched off but before they reached the other side), a great windstorm hit the lake. Remember, this is a lake, not a sea or an ocean, which means this is a smaller body of water. They are on a lake; not the largest body of water they will cross, but still a nice sized body of water. A great windstorm comes on the lake and tosses so much water in the boat; tosses the boat so much that they were in real jeopardy of dying. The Scripture doesn't say "they thought they were perishing", it says "they were perishing".

Since Jesus' disciples were on the boat, and we know that at least four of His disciples were fishermen by trade (Peter, Andrew, James and John), we know that there were at least four men on that boat who knew naturally, what to do when a windstorm hit the body of water they were on. This means that they must have been in the middle of the lake; too far away from the other side for comfort, yet too deep in to go back. A windstorm on a lake that fills up a boat with enough water, that caused an experienced crew thought they were about to die, sounds like an incredibly big and/or violent storm to me. This whole scene brings to mind the kind of storm that we see in movies.

The disciples, fearing for their lives, go to Jesus and wake Him up telling Him that they are perishing. Jesus is not disturbed. Jesus is in the boat with them, undoubtably soaked with water and feeling the tossing of the boat in the waves like they are, but He is undisturbed. When they awaken Jesus, He gets up and rebukes the wind (the unseen root cause) and the raging of the water (the physical thing that is affected by the unseen wind), and they both cease- the wind and the raging water. Then Jesus does something interesting, He turns to them and rebukes them and says, *"Where is your faith"*.

The fact that Jesus asks them 'where was their faith', means that this was a problem that they could have solved themselves. Understand the train of thought; when Jesus told them to go to the other side and got in the boat with them, not only did they have the power to complete the task simply because He had spoken the Word, but He was also in the boat with them, which was double proof that the Word spoken could and would be accomplished. Jesus would not tell them to do what could not be accomplished, and surely as a man anointed with the Spirit of God and on an assignment from God, He would not perish before His assignment was completed. Therefore, when Jesus gave them the Word (command) to go to the other side and went to sleep leaving them in charge of completing the task, they were endowed with the power to complete the task no matter what situation came up.

For the disciples, the situation that came up threatening to stop them from completing the task Jesus had given them, was the very real threat of death from an unseen force. They could not see the wind itself; they could only see and feel the effects the wind had on the physical things around them; the clouds, the lightning, the water and the boat. These natural threats were causing them to fear death to their natural bodies. However, they had the power to speak to an unseen force; stopping it from having an effect on the natural forces that was causing them to fear death and stopping them from reaching the other side. This is why Jesus rebuked them saying, "Where is your faith."

It is the same way for us in our businesses and our lives. When God gives us a command on what to do, He has not only given us the power to complete the task, but He has also given us the power by His Spirit to rebuke the unseen forces that would affect the natural things surrounding us that speaks of death- our death and/or the death of the purpose of God. When you have received a Word from God about what He has for you; what He has given you and what He wants you to do, you have been given the power to overcome the seen and unseen forces that would attempt to abort that Word. Not only can you speak to seen and unseen forces, you are expected to do it by and in faith. You cannot die in the middle of the assignment (lake) unless you lack faith, do not believe or are in blatant disobedience.

Had the disciples operated in faith, they never would have been in physical jeopardy, because they would have spoken to the wind well before it got to the point of potential death. If you believe the Word that God has given you and move in faith, then you must reach the other side.

Here is the thing though; we walk by faith not by sight. We live by faith; which means we live by every Word that proceeds from the mouth of our God. We are not to be disobedient in any area of our lives. When we are completely obedient and surrendered to God in every area of our lives, satan has noting in us. When we live in obedience, we live in faith; God is the hedge of protection around us and our shield from everything. When we dwell in the secret place of the Most High (in Christ), we abide under the shadow of the Almighty, and nothing by any means can harm us. If you are securely in Him and walking in the Word of your assignment, not even death can do you any harm.

This is the anointed entrepreneur; the son and daughter of the kingdom that has heard a Word from God concerning taking the kingdoms (industries) of this world for the kingdom of God. The anointed entrepreneur hears the Word and knows that nothing can stop them from completing that Word. The anointed entrepreneur knows that even opposition from unseen forces that wreak havoc upon the physical things of this world to the point that death is present, that opposition cannot stop them because the power to rebuke both the unseen and seen forces of opposition was given to them when they were given the command to 'go to the other side".

The Children of Israel
When God spoke to Moses to have the children of Israel begin to possess the land that He was giving to them, God had them cross over water as well. In order to reach the promised land, in order to take possession of the land that God has given to you, you are going to have to go through the water (the Word). You are going to have to leave the land that you know, and cross over into the place where God is sending you.

> *"Rise, take your journey, and cross over the River Arnon. Look, I have given into your hand Sihon the Amorite, king of Heshbon, and his land. Begin to possess it, and engage him in battle. This day I will begin to put the fear of you upon the nations under the whole heaven, who shall hear the report of you and shall tremble and be in anguish because of you." (Deuteronomy 2:2,25 NKJV).*

(This is a prophetic Word for right now to those who have ears to hear.)

When God sent the children of Israel over the River Arnon, He gave them great victory over Sihon the Amorite, king of Heshbon and over Og king of Bashan. The children of Israel defeated these two kings, dispossessed them and all of their people, and then possessed their land in their place. However, the work was not done. Some would look at these two victories and think that God has done a great work through them, and relax in the luxury of what was taken. As we read further, we find out that the two lands that they had just taken was not even the tip of the iceberg compared to what God had purposed to give to them.

> "Then I commanded you at that time, saying: 'The
> Lord your God has given you this land to possess.
> All of you men of valor shall cross over armed
> before your brethren, the children of Israel. But
> your wives, your little ones and your livestock (I
> know that you have much livestock) shall stay in
> your cities which I have given you, until the Lord has
> given rest to your brethren as to you, and they also
> possess the land which the Lord your God is giving
> to them beyond the Jordan. Then each of you may
> return to his possession which I have given to you."
> (Deuteronomy 3:18-20 NKJV)

As an anointed entrepreneur, the goal is not to possess your land and stop to enjoy it. You are the mighty men of valor; you are God's warriors that is taking back what the enemy has stolen. You are to continue to fight until your brothers and sisters are possessing their land as well. There should not be one child of God that is in lack; all of God's people have been given land in Christ Jesus. Some people will continue to fight to dispossess more land, some will live in the land to keep possession of it, but all are to have their land.

When the children of Israel conquered a land, they were told to leave nothing alive; tear down the idols, and kill every man, woman and child and possess all of the land in their place. As an anointed entrepreneur, you are to do the same thing. No, we are not to physically kill anyone, but we are supposed to tear down the idols, dispossess the people in that land and possess in its place. We should be taking over businesses and industries (dispossessing) and replacing the people in it (possessing) with children of the kingdom.

We are kingdom people, and who are our brothers, sisters and mothers? Our brothers, sisters and mothers are other kingdom citizens. The righteous cannot be forsaken and we are to be putting kingdom citizens in their place; putting each other in positions of power and doing business with kingdom citizens. This is the will of God.

Undoubtably, there will be many who read this word and say, "that seems wrong; after all, people who are not saved have families they need to feed to. Why should I go into the land and possess it and take out the people already there? Shouldn't I let the people who are currently in the land stay and possess it with me? Shouldn't we all be friends?"

Child of God, friendship with the world is enmity with God. God has never directed His people to possess His promises with those that are not His people. Yes, you are to minister to the unsaved, but possession of the land is a promise given to the sons and daughters of the kingdom of heaven. Nowhere in the Scripture are God's people told to possess the land and leave the people that are in the land where they are. God separates the wheat from the tares, the children of the kingdom of light from the children of the kingdom of darkness.

> *"Do not be unequally yoked together with*
> *unbelievers. For what fellowship has righteousness*
> *with lawlessness? And what communion has light*
> *with darkness? And what accord has Christ with*
> *Belial? Or what part has a believer with an unbeliever?*
> *And what agreement has the temple of God with*
> *idols? For you are the temple of the living God. As*
> *God has said; 'I will dwell in them and walk among*
> *them. I will be their God and they shall be My*
> *people.' Therefore 'Come out from among them and*

*be separate, says the Lord. Do not touch what is
unclean, and I will receive you. I will be a Father to
you, and you shall be My sons and daughters, Says the
Lord Almighty.'" (2 Corinthians 6:14-18 NKJV)*

For an anointed entrepreneur, your business will stay anointed in
every area if you have other anointed people placed in leadership
position in your business. Anointed people hear from God and
obey God. Anointed people are planted by God; and everything
their hands touch prospers- this is a promise from God. Anointed
people hear from the Holy Spirit, who tells us of things to come.
God reveals wisdom and revelation to anointed people. Anointed
people have life and have it more abundantly. How much could
God accomplish through the entrepreneur who is anointed and
submitted to the Lord in every area of their business? How many
people could God reach through the business that is wholly
obedient and connected to Him? If your finance department or
sales department or human resources department or any other
department is not being run by a child of the kingdom of God, you
can and will suffer loss, because the blessing of God is not on the
unrighteous but on the righteous. As an anointed entrepreneur, if
you want someone in particular to work with you in your
business, lead them to Christ.

I hear some of you saying, "there are laws against rejecting
someone for a job based on their religious beliefs." Yes, there are.
But there is no law stopping you from asking God to send the
person He has ordained to fill a particular position to you. There is
no law against listening to the Spirit of God when it is time to
choose who to hire for a particular business. There is no law
against doing business with other kingdom entrepreneurs. What I
am saying is that if God gave you the business, He has walked out
the entire thing. He has people he has ordained to fill all the
positions that need to be filled, so that He can take you into all of
the land He has given you.

"And you shall remember the Lord your God, for it is

He who gives you the power to get wealth, that He
may establish His covenant which He swore to your
fathers, as it were to this day."
(Deuteronomy 8:18 NKJV)

God is establishing you and your business so that He may establish His covenant which He swore. Who are the covenant people of God? The covenant people of God are the people who have accepted the Son of God, Jesus Christ; those are the people whom God is in covenant with. The sons of the kingdom of God are the ones who carry the covenant, promises, glory and blessings of God...no others. Therefore, it would seem like wisdom to dispossess those that have the curse on them and let the blessed, the righteousness of God in Christ Jesus to possess in their place.

There is only one way to guarantee that the blessing of God is on every area of your business; make sure that you have sons and daughters of the kingdom in every area of your business.

Selah.

Section C
WAR

Preface

Most of us never consider that when we open a business, as a citizen of the kingdom of heaven, we are going to war. Everything we do as citizens of the kingdom of heaven is met in war. The enemy of our faith has declared war with us. The devil and the fallen angels that make up the principalities, powers, rulers of the darkness of this age, spiritual wickedness in heavenly places, thrones, dominions, all the disembodied spirits of wickedness, every man, woman, child and beast that is working in conjunction with lucifer and the fallen angels have declared war against the redeemed of God. We are admonished by Paul in Scripture to 'walk by faith and not by sight' because 'the just live by faith'. We also must not ignore the Apostle Paul when he tells us to 'fight *the good fight of faith'*. On this earth, faith in the Word of God will be a constant fight.

The blessed thing to know is that God has given us the tools and weapons we need to maintain the victory that we received in and through Christ Jesus. When Jesus came, He was on a mission to destroy the works of the devil. Destruction of the devil's kingdom does not occur by happenstance; it is a purposeful activity that is continuous with us.

Just as Jesus declared, "I AM", we are *'in Jesus Name'*; we live, move and have our being in Jesus' Name. Everywhere we see the marks and residue of the devil's work (stealing, killing and destroying), we are to destroy his works in the power of Jesus' Name. We are more than conquerors, because our Lord and Savior has already won the victory; He has defeated the devil, made an open spectacle of the kingdom and power of darkness and given that victory and His Name to us not only to maintain His victory, but to expand the kingdom of God.

> *"And you, being dead in your trespasses and the*
> *uncircumcision of your flesh, He has made alive*
> *together with Him, having forgiven you all*
> *trespasses, having wiped out the handwriting*
> *or requirements that was against us, which was*
> *contrary to us. And He has taken it out of the way,*
> *having nailed it to the cross. Having disarmed*
> *principalities and powers, He made a public*
> *spectacle of them, triumphing over them in it."*
> *(Colossians 2:13-15 NKJV)*

Jesus came to show us the Father. Jesus is the 'author and finisher of our faith', meaning that His walk on the earth shows us how a man filled with the Spirit of the living God is to operate (live) by faith, on this earth. Jesus is the finisher of our faith, because He has completed the plan of God and obtained victory on our behalf through the cross and the shedding of His blood for us. That is why we are told to *'let this mind be in you that was also in Christ Jesus"*. We are not merely walking on the earth using the Name of Jesus, we are walking this earth *'in the Name of Jesus'*.

Jesus walked in continuous victory; He met every challenge and every battle that came to Him and won. Where the devil and the kingdom of darkness caused sickness, disease and deformities, Jesus destroyed their works. Where the devil and the kingdom of darkness had stolen the joy, peace, connection to God, and the knowledge of God the Father, Jesus restored it. Where the devil and the kingdom of darkness used death to rule over people to cause them to fear and be estranged from their heavenly Father who loved them, Jesus took back the keys to death, hell and the grave and gives life to all who believe in Him.

As an anointed entrepreneur you are at war; your business is born in war. Every piece of land (industry) you take on this earth by the power of and in the Name of Jesus, is taken through war- and you must maintain it through war. The enemy and the kingdom of darkness will constantly and consistently try to cause you to doubt, fail and shut down; they are not playing with you. The enemy of your faith does not want you to help people nor become prosperous in a world system that he is the god of. The enemy does not want you to have the power to get wealth so that God can establish His covenant which He swore. The devil and the kingdom of darkness wants you 'broke, busted and disgusted'.

However, the will of God for your life and your business is to be victorious, blessed and always increasing. God wants you to have provision so you can support the kingdom ("that there will be meat in My house"), so you can support your family, and that you can bring other sons and daughters into the kingdom and into their land. Our Father wants you to do good works in the Name of Jesus that will cause people to glorify our Father which is in heaven. This is why God gives you, the anointed entrepreneur, the power to get wealth; so that He may established His covenant which He swore to our Fathers of faith.

Chapter Fifteen
Keys to the Kingdom

In Matthew Chapter 16, we learn of some of the power we have been given by Jesus, because of God's revelation to us of who Jesus is. In Matthew Chapter 16, Jesus was having a conversation with His disciples about who He is;

> "When Jesus came into the region of Caesarea
> Philippi, He asked His disciples, saying, 'Who do
> men say that I, the Son of Man, am?' So they
> said, 'Some say John the Baptist, some Elijah,
> and others Jeremiah or one of the prophets.'
> He said to them, 'But who do you say that I am?'"

(Matthew 16:13-15 NKJV)

Let's stop here for a moment; this is the first realization that we must come to in order to operate in the kingdom of heaven. At some point in our walk, we must all come to the understanding of who the world says that Jesus is and who we have decided that Jesus is. The reason we must confront these questions is because what the world says and what we decide is going to put us either in friendship with the world (which is enmity with God), or it is going to set us up for war from that moment on.

When we agree with what the world say about Jesus the Christ; that He was merely a prophet, an enlightened person, just a good man, an historical figure, a liar, some guy who is dead or that He never existed, we have become a friend of the world and are at that moment, at enmity with God. For definition's sake, the word enmity as defined in the dictionary means, *'the state or feeling of being actively opposed or hostile to someone or something.'* When we side with the world, we are actually being hostile towards God. We are calling Him a liar; which even most people in this natural world consider disrespectful enough to fight you over.

Once we define who men say that Jesus is, the next obvious question is, *'who do we personally say that Jesus is?'* This is the million-dollar question; no question on earth is as important as this question. We all have to make a personal decision on who we say that Jesus, the Christ of God is, every single day. Are we going to agree with what God has said about Jesus, or are we going to agree with what other men say about Jesus?

The thing is, you cannot know who Jesus is apart from revelation from God. The way our Father designed salvation to happen, is for it to be shared by His redeemed through their words.

> *"Now all things are of God, who has reconciled us to Himself through Jesus Christ, and has given to us the ministry of reconciliation, that is, that God was*

in Christ reconciling the world to Himself, not
imputing their trespasses to them, and has
committed to us the word of reconciliation. Now
then, we are ambassadors for Christ, as though
God were pleading through us; we implore you on
Christ's behalf, be reconciled to God."
(2 Corinthians 5:18-20 NKJV)

and,

"For the message of the cross is foolishness to those
who are perishing, but to us who are being saved it
is the power of God. For it is written: 'I will destroy
the wisdom of the wise, and bring to nothing the
understanding of the prudent.' Where is the wise?
Where is the scribe? Where is the disputer of this
age? Has not God made foolish the wisdom of the
world? For since, in the wisdom of God, the world
through wisdom did not know God, it pleased God
through the foolishness of the message preached
to save those who believe."
(1 Corinthians 1:18-21 NKJV)

The message of Jesus being the Christ of God is shared by His redeemed ones. Once the Word of God about Jesus Christ is shared, we are told that God reveals the person of the Son of God to the individual; so that they can know Jesus as the Christ. Our Father gives us the *'measure of faith to believe.'* Once the Son of God is revealed to the heart of man, then that man or women must confess that Jesus is Lord *(agree with their mouth in the earth about what God has said about Jesus in the heavens),* -and must believe in their heart that God has raised this same Jesus from the dead *(hence Jesus becoming the acceptable sacrifice to God for man's sins so that man can be reconciled to a Holy God).* Then that revelation of the truth can believed by the individual. *"But who do you say that I am?"*

Once an individual receives revelation that Jesus is the Christ and accepts that, then God can speak to them and tell them who they are. God does this through revelation as well;

> *"Jesus therefore answered them and said to them, 'Do not murmur among yourselves. No one can come to Me unless the Father who sent Me draws him; and I will raise him up at the last day. It is written in the prophets, "And they shall be taught by God." Therefore everyone who has heard and learned from the Father comes to Me.'"*
> *(John 6:43-45 NKJV)*

Jesus can then reveal to us that we are in Him, Christ Jesus. Jesus reveals that we are the righteousness of God in Him, and that He has empowered us to complete an assignment in His Name. All of these things come through revelation. Jesus tells us;

> *"Blessed are you, Simon Bar-Jonah, for flesh and blood has not revealed this to you, but My Father who is in heaven. And I say to you that you are Peter, and on this rock I will build My church and the gates of Hades shall not prevail against it. And I will give to you the keys of the kingdom of heaven, and whatsoever you bind on earth will be bound in heaven, and whatever you loose on earth will be loosed in heaven."*
> *(Matthew 16:17-19 NKJV)*

This is the important part for your business; when God reveals Jesus to you, the next thing Jesus does is reveal who you are in Christ. The rock that Jesus builds His church on is revelation; revelation from God to you about Jesus and then revelation from Jesus to you about who you are in Him. This is how we understand who we are in Christ (a new creation) and what He has called us to do in Christ.

Jesus promised to do this; so if you do not know what you are to do, you have to go back to the source, and receive revelation from Jesus about yourself. If your assignment is in business, that means God has shown you that Jesus is His Son in whom all things consists, and Jesus has shown you that you are anointed and empowered by Him to accomplish the purposes of God on this earth. Jesus reveals to you that you are an anointed business person, empowered to do business in His Name on this earth so that God can be glorified in the Son. You cannot fail because Jesus has revealed the heart of God to you and God cannot fail.

Once you know from Jesus that your business is purposed and anointed by Him, you understand that you have the power and the authority to move mountains, dispossess the enemy, possess the land and get wealth so that God may establish His covenant which He swore. As long as you live and operate by the revelation of the authority and power you have received from Jesus through the Spirit of God, you cannot fail and no man will be able to stand before you all the days of your life. Just as God was with Moses and with Jesus, Jesus and the Father will be with you through His Holy Spirit. You cannot lose, you cannot fail. The very gates of Hades will not prevail against you because you are the church; the very body of Jesus on the earth. Gates are motionless objects, whose purpose is generally to keep you out and prevent you from accessing a certain area. Jesus says the gates of Hades itself, which is set up to prevent the anointed entrepreneur from coming in to take over the industries/kingdoms of this world's system, will not prevail in keeping you out.

As an anointed entrepreneur, Jesus has given you the power and authority to kick down the gates of Hades and possess the land beyond these gates. Doesn't that excite you? There is nowhere the soles of your feet cannot tread (no industry or worldly system), and God has promised that everywhere the soles of your feet do tread upon, He has given it to you.

Furthermore, Jesus promised to give you the keys to the kingdom of heaven. What are these keys good for? The keys to the kingdom of heaven are good for binding and loosing on earth what has been bound and loosed in heaven. These keys refer to pieces of wisdom that is revealed to us from Jesus about how the kingdom of heaven operates in this physical world.

I will give you a key of the kingdom of heaven for an anointed entrepreneur right now;

*One Key of the kingdom of heaven
We are not supposed to toil for our businesses to become rich when we are anointed entrepreneurs. Toil is the way that people get rich in this world, using the world's system of monetary gain. In this world's system you are supposed to get loans to start up your business, and work your fingers to the bone to pay back loans (making the banks richer) and spend a large portion of your income to pay people to run your business (or spend all your time running the business). You are supposed to sacrifice your one life on this earth for your business, so you can perhaps have a nice house, a car and pay your bills; so that the mortgage holder, the car companies, the credit card companies, the utility companies and other billing companies can get richer. Of all the unsaved people that start a business in the world and work their life to maintain that business, trying to get rich, only a very small percentage of them ever reach the status of wealth that allows them to retire (and stay retired); living the rest of their lives without worry. That is the way the world operates. But the Scripture tells the anointed entrepreneur;

> *"Do not overwork to be rich; because of your own understanding, cease! Will you set your eyes on that which is not? For riches certainly make themselves wings: they fly away like an eagle toward heaven." (Proverbs 23:4,5 NKJV)*

and;

> *"Trust in the Lord with all your heart, and lean not on your own understanding; in all your ways acknowledge Him, and He shall direct your paths." (Proverbs 3:5,6 NKJV)*

and;

> *"Wisdom is the principal thing; therefore get wisdom. And in all your getting, get understanding. Exalt her, and she will promote you; she will bring you honor, when you embrace her. She will place on your head an ornament of grace; a crown of glory she will deliver you." (Proverbs 4:7-9 NKJV)*

In the kingdom of God, we do not toil for wealth and riches; we seek wisdom from God and trust His Word. I will give you a real-world example.

Personal Testimony of an Anointed Entrepreneur
I have had a number of businesses that I have opened over the years; and all of them failed to make any substantial money. I worked so very hard, and never saw any abundance for my efforts. When I moved to Virginia, I wanted to open a business so I opened a movie rental store. I dumped thousands of dollars in that store, well over ten thousand dollars. I believe that all in all I made maybe two thousand dollars in that store, which went to bills. My wife and I spent seven days a week in that store (until she bailed on me and got a real job); we stayed in that store from 10:00 am usually to 9:00 pm, even later on the weekends. We hardly ever had any customers; Netflix had just come on the market and was taking over everything.

Right before the business shut down, I got something in the mail saying I could take a Jackson Hewitt class for free to learn to do taxes. I am a nerd and always liked doing taxes. I figured that I could take the class, learn the business and add it to the movie rental store so I could make some money. Maybe I could even open my own tax business one day.

I took the tax class at Jackson Hewitt, and when I finished my training, I turned down their little eight dollar an hour job offer because I felt I could add a tax service to my movie rental business and make my own money. I tried that, but I could not get enough clients to save the business. Withing a year, I shut down the movie business, took all of the videos I had purchased and sold them for pennies on the dollar at the flea market just to recoup some of my money. I cried about my bad decision for a while, and tried to plan something that would work.

The next tax season, a friend of mine who was working at a check cashing and money lending business called me and said, "I know you learned how to do taxes, would you like to come do taxes for our company?" This was God directing me, but I didn't know it at the time. All I knew was I needed to make some money, so I took the job. My friend didn't work there long after I started, but I developed a relationship with everyone at the business and continued to work there for the next three tax seasons; running the tax portion of the business by myself. God had put me in a position to learn how to run a tax business, and I was still clueless.

Soon I had to leave there because I felt they were cheating me out of my money. That next tax season I took a position at Liberty Tax. It was great and terrible at the same time. It was great because I was making more money, but after being with them for a little while, I was discouraged by what I considered to be bad business practices. It seemed to me that the company was charging the poorest of people, four and five hundred dollars to do their taxes and not giving them good service or the respect I felt they deserved. After my second year working with them, I decided I could and would do a better job on my own; I was dedicated to learning the business, I would respect the people and I wouldn't overcharge them for the service I provided.

I started looking into starting my own tax business but was discouraged quickly. In order to rent a space in a decent location, I would have to spend between $1,500 - $1,800 a month in rent alone. Then, when I added other things like desks, chairs, furniture, computers, servers, marketing, signage, employees, insurance, utilities, marketing and other things (for a business that was only open from January to April), I saw that it would cost me $40,000 - $50,000 just to start that business; and that was before I did one tax return. I thought, "do you know how many tax returns I would have to do and at what price I would have to charge to make that money back my in first year?" I didn't have access to that type of money and my credit was mud, so I knew no bank would lend me that money, and I didn't know anyone that I could ask to invest in me. I was done before I ever started.

I did the only thing I could; I cried- but this time I cried out to God to help me. I cried to God to show me how to open the tax business. God is so faithful, merciful and full of Grace. At the time I wasn't living right, I wasn't abiding in His Word and letting His Word abide in me. However, when I called out to Jesus to save me and help me, He did just that. What I later realized is, what I needed was not money, but wisdom. The scripture says;

> *"You lust and do not have. You murder and covet*
> *and cannot obtain. You fight and war. Yet you do*
> *not have because you do not ask. You ask and do*
> *not receive, because you ask amiss, that you may*
> *spend it on your own pleasures."*
> *(James 4:2-4 NKJV)*

As an anointed entrepreneur, you must seek God. God is your Father and He wants you to be blessed and He wants to give you the kingdom. Also realize, if you are asking for the wrong things, you cannot receive the anointed thing. God was so merciful to me because at the time I did not know the things in this book. I asked God, "how do I do it, how do I create this business?" I didn't ask Him for the money, because I honestly didn't believe I could get the money. I just asked for a way; basically, I sought God for wisdom.

What God did is give me wisdom. I began to think, "well people don't like going to the tax office anyway; children running around wiping their hands on their noses and touching everything, it's winter and people come in coughing and not covering their mouths, everyone is sitting so close together at the tax desk that the next person can hear all your business and the tax preparers don't study their craft, so they do little more that data entry. Maybe I don't need a tax office." God revealed to me that I could use the computer in my house, put the tax software on it and do taxes from my home with the people I knew.

I purchased the tax software I had been using at the first tax job I had and my wife got me a few clients from people she knew at her job. My first year in business, I had five clients and made over one thousand dollars. Then I asked God how to get more clients for the next year. He told me to tell all five of my clients that if they referred someone to me, I would pay them $50 cash. I did that and the next tax season my client based doubled. The third year my client base doubled again and now I was making decent money. For the fourth year, God told me to get a laptop and a printer and make my business mobile and I did. My clientele continued to grow; for the first five years my client base doubled until I was doing very well. I was spending the money on things that was not netting me back any money, but that was another lesson I had to learn.

After five years, I saw that I needed to grow up and change the things I was spending my money on, so my family could really increase. I thought about opening an office again, but I didn't want to spend that type of money; the way I was doing taxes now kept my expenses down to much less than ten percent of what I made, and I didn't have to spend money until I made money.

I have been operating my tax business as a mobile business for 11 years. Over these years, I have kept my overhead down to less than five percent of my income, purchased income producing real estate for cash, paid off all our debt, taken my wife on multiple vacations each year and not had to work a job for the rest of the year after tax season; which allowed me to invest in and try new businesses. God has truly been good.

The point is; an anointed entrepreneur does not operate in business the way the world does. We are given direct revelation from our God on how to do certain things, which causes us not to have to toil in order to receive our promotion and increase. As we obey God's Word and seek Him before we make our decisions, Jesus promised us that He would give us the keys to the kingdom of heaven so we can get things done. As we use these divine keys, we can kick down any gate that hades has constructed, and possess more land. We are promised that He will be with us always, and that He will never leave us nor forsake us. God has promised us that no man will be able to stand before us all the days of our lives.

The anointed entrepreneur has a Scripture full of promises to lean on, so that we can complete the plans and purposes of our Holy God who has gone before us and fought the battle for us, and then walks with us as we possess the land that He has given to us.

You are not an entrepreneur; you are an anointed entrepreneur, there is a difference.

Word from The Lord:
A Key to the Kingdom from the Spirit of God
As I was praying this morning, I clearly heard the Spirit of the Lord speaking to me, a key to the kingdom of God for His people in

general, the anointed entrepreneur specifically. This is what the Lord Jehovah Most High is saying to you;

"Seek Me. Acknowledging Me in all your ways means not just prayer, but in reading My Word. Many of you are making the wrong decisions and do not walk in the fullness of what I have designed for you, because you are not seeking Me properly. Yes, you pray and yes you ask questions, but you are not getting complete answers. Why? Because you are not following up with the reading of My Word. My Word is a light unto your path; the light and revelation comes through My complete Word, not just the rhema but the logos. I speak through My Word. It is not just about the particular Scripture that you are reading; when you read My Word, I can speak to you, truth. When you are reading My Word the Holy Spirit can search out the deep things and reveal them to you, because you are in communion with Me at that moment. I am the Lord Your God, and I long to give you the power that you need to achieve your goal, and no good thing will I withhold to those who are found in Me. My Son has said, 'if you abide in Me and MY WORD abides in you, you will ask what you will, and it will be done for you.' But this abiding in My Word means reading it, consuming it until you are speaking it. When you are consumed with a subject that is all you talk about. Remember when you were infatuated with a member of the opposite sex or with sports or other natural things; that is all you could talk about, that is all you spent your time on. Be the same way with My Word, and then you will speak a thing and it will be established for you, then you will say to this mountain, "Be thou removed and cast into the sea" and it will happen. Seek My Word and you will be established, because you will know My Word and it will permeate your natural being until you are continuously walking in My Spirit of Truth."

Obtaining Wisdom and Understanding
The question comes to mind, "how exactly does one obtain wisdom and understanding?" If the Scripture says *"Wisdom is the principle thing therefore get wisdom, and in all your getting get*

understanding", then it follows that the Scripture should tell us exactly what wisdom and understanding are as well as how to get wisdom and how to get understanding.

To start, we find a beginning definition of wisdom in Proverbs 9:10-12;

> *"The fear of the Lord is the beginning of wisdom;*
> *and the knowledge of the Holy One is*
> *understanding. For by me your days will be*
> *multiplied, and years of your life will be added to*
> *you. If you are wise, you are wise for yourself,*
> *and if you scoff, you will bear it alone." (NKJV)*

Wisdom only comes from one place and that is our God. Also, see in these verses that there is a difference between having wisdom and being wise. Once you possess (live out) the fear of the Lord (reverence of, knowledge of the Lord as the One true God), that is the beginning of wisdom. There is no way to obtain wisdom without the fear of the Lord because the Lord God Himself is wisdom, which He reveals to us through His Word.

Understand, the fear of the Lord is only the beginning of wisdom because you must first believe that 'God is' and then that He is a rewarder of those who diligently seek Him. Again; what is the reward for diligently seeking Him? The reward for diligently seeking God is finding God; the Lord God becoming your father, your protector, your exceeding great reward. Our God becomes all of these things and so much more through His Word. Once you begin to fear the Lord and acknowledge Him as God, then He will begin to reveal His Word in your life, which is wisdom being downloaded to you. God will direct your paths, which means He will reveal to you the right paths to take. The Holy Spirit will tell you of things to come which is wisdom being downloaded to you.

Understanding is seen through your knowledge of the Holy One. Once you know Christ Jesus, you have understanding;

understanding of spiritual things, understanding of the mystery that has been kept secret since the foundation of the earth which is Christ Jesus in us. That is understanding. See we often think of things just from a natural perspective, but we are not natural; we are living spirits (unto God), with the breath of the Almighty God in us as we walk about in natural bodies on this physical earth. We are supernatural because we are alive to Christ. Understanding is knowing that we live, move and have our being in Christ Jesus; which means that everything is under the dictate and control of our Father. All things must work for the good of those who are called according to His purpose. We are more than conquerors though Christ Jesus and, in the end, we win because God will keep all that which is submitted to Him until the very end of the age; and after the end of the age we will have life everlasting and be with Him forever. This is understanding because it frames our perspective both in the natural and in the spiritual; we serve the only true and living God and all things are sustained and upheld by the power of His Word.

Being wise is nothing like having wisdom. Being wise is an earthly attribute that comes through experience. Experience (either first hand or second hand) tells us not to play with fire because we will get burned. Experience tells us that everyone that smiles in your face is not your friend. Those who learn natural things must learn them through experience; either something they personally have experienced or something they had the sense enough to believe by being told from someone else who has personally experienced it. Being wise is merely earthly experience and it is mostly sensual; you do not perceive to be wise; you have to experience it or believe someone else who has experienced it. It is possible to be wise and not have wisdom, because wisdom is not sensual; it does not come from experience, but from God.

Consider Solomon, the wisest person that lived. Solomon received wisdom straight from God. Solomon knew things that he had not learned from experience; he was able to judge things that he had not experienced. For example, in 1 Kings 3:16-27, we read of a situation that King Solomon judged over in which wisdom was seen.

Two women who lived together gave birth to children three days apart. One of the children died in the night and the mother of the dead child snuck over to the other mother, took her living child and placed the dead child on her chest while she slept. In the morning the mother who now had the dead child on her chest went to feed the child and noticed the child was dead. The grief she must have felt in that moment.

However, while grieving over the dead child, she noticed something wrong. The mother started inspecting the child and realized that the dead child she was holding was not her child at all. Immediately she looked to her roommate, saw that child and knew exactly what happened; the children had been switched! As you can imagine, she was livid. There was no peace in that house; in fact, there was such a quarrel that the matter was brought before King Solomon, the supreme court if you will.

After hearing the story and witnessing both women screaming that the living child was theirs, King Solomon came up with a solution. He ordered a sword be brough to him and told his guards to take the sword and divide the child in half and give half to each who claimed the child was theirs. Brilliant! The mother who already had a dead child would not care if this child was killed also, because her child was already dead, and we all know (through experience), misery loves company.

Of course, the real mother of the living child did not want to see the child killed. The mother of the living child, who yearned with compassion for her son said, *"O my lord, give her the living child, and by no means kill him!"* King Solomon automatically knew whose child it was because of the compassion.

This is wisdom. You cannot come to a decision like this through experience but through wisdom; insight and revelation from God on what to do in a specific situation- and you can only get this type of on the spot wisdom from understanding- knowing God, His voice and His heart. There is another scripture in Proverbs which says;

> "The ear that hears the rebukes of life will abide
> among the wise. He who disdains instruction
> despises his own soul, but he who heeds rebuke
> gets understanding. The fear of the Lord is the
> instruction of wisdom, and before honor is
> humility." (Proverbs 15: 31-33 NKJV)

We see here that the rebukes of life, or the learned experiences taught by earthly lessons make a person wise; and that heeding the lessons taught through these experiences will allow you to understand the benefits of the earthly lessons learned. In contrast, the fear of the Lord is the instruction of wisdom; wisdom comes from reverencing God alone. The fear of the Lord are the lessons that give a person wisdom; revelation and information that is not subject to personal experience.

As an anointed entrepreneur you need wisdom, not to be wise. As an entrepreneur, experience with making bad decisions that causes loss (of money, time, energy, etc.) makes you wise in business, but it is painful and can be deadly to your business. On the other hand, the fear of the Lord, which leads to revelation straight from God, will change your operating mindset and cause you to avoid the decision and situations which cause loss.

Would you prefer to be an entrepreneur or an anointed entrepreneur? Would you like to be wise and learn through earthly experience or would you like to have wisdom and learn through direct revelation from God? The choice is always yours, and the choice is always continual, this is why the Scriptures say;

> "Trust in the Lord with all your heart and lean not
> on your own understanding. In all your ways

acknowledge Him and He shall direct your paths."
(Proverbs 3:5,6 NKJV)

Anointed entrepreneurs, for your own sake, trust in the Lord. This is a daily walk and work. Lean not on your own understanding which comes through earthly experience; acknowledge Him, fear Him, reverence Him, seek Him in all your ways and He shall direct your paths. Our Father will give you wisdom to make the correct and profitable decision, which will give you peace, not evil, and give you an expected, good and profitable end.

Chapter Sixteen
The enemy

War; we are at war I tell you.

As anointed entrepreneurs, we sometimes forget that we are at war. We think that we are here on earth doing business like everyone else. We look at our businesses as merely corporations, LLC's, sole proprietorships, non-profit corporations or other man-made entities in a man-made system, which is controlled and dictated to by the god of this world. We, as anointed entrepreneurs, forget that we are supernatural; new creations of God Almighty Himself, made to live in this world, but not according to the dictates of this world.

We are anointed by God, and we have a calling to dispossess the enemy and possess the land created and given to us by God in the place of the enemy. We are commanded to, and endowed with the power to get wealth, so that God may establish the covenant that He spoke to His faithful servants. We are called to receive the wealth of the wicked that is stored up for the just, so that we can build the kingdom of God and destroy the works of the devil.

We are at war; yet we are more than conquerors because Jesus is alive. Jesus has overcome death, hell and the grave and is sitting at the right hand of God. Jesus has obtained the victory over satan. We are to maintain and expand what He has accomplished in His Name. This is not the time for sporting cars or hording homes or anything else temporal; this is the time for advancing the kingdom of God and the purposes of God until Jesus our Lord, Savior and King returns to rule forever.

If we as anointed entrepreneur are at war, we must understand a few things. First, our enemies are not other men and women on this earth;

> *"For we wrestle not against flesh and blood, but*
> *against principalities, against powers, against the*
> *rulers of the darkness of this age, against spiritual*
> *hosts of wickedness in the heavenly places."*
> *(Ephesians 6:12 NKJV)*

As an anointed entrepreneur you must understand that you will have to war to start, grow and expand your business. An anointed entrepreneur knows the true purpose behind the business and land that they are possessing; to do the will of God and advance the kingdom of God. Just as with the children of Israel, every piece of land you take because of the promise of God will come with a battle. The physical battles we read of in Joshua, as God lead His people in the taking of the land that He had promised to give them, every single inch that they possessed came through a battle, and an overthrowing of the enemy that lived there.

Although God promised His people that He had given them the land and promised to help them take it, they still had to fight for every inch. God was with them, and they eventually took all of the land that God had promised them by dispossessing the enemy who was already there, but every inch was a battle, because the enemy did not merely give it up when they walked in.

All of the scripture is for our understanding of who our God is and how He operates. The same way that God's people fought for and won the battles necessary to inherit the promises our Father gave to them, we will obtain and receive the promises of our Father in the same way. Jesus came to show us how the anointed man, filled with the Spirit of the Living God, walks this earth destroying the works of the devil and submitting to God even unto the point of death. Jesus is the way; He has shown us the way and He has become our way to fulfill the Word of God on this earth. Jesus shows us that not only is our fight a spiritual fight (as opposed to the physical one that the children of Israel had in the old testament), He also shows us how we win this Spiritual fight; by abiding in Him- believing His Word and walking it out by faith.

Our fight is not the same as the fight that the children of Israel had in the old testament, although we are still fighting to obtain the land that God has given us through His promises. We are told by Jesus, that as we fight and obtain the promises of God, "the gates of hell shall not prevail against us". Everywhere the soles of our feet tread we can have, because the protections and defenses that the kingdom of darkness has set up to keep us out, will not prevail in keeping us out. We kick through and down the gates protecting the land that the kingdom of darkness currently has claim to, and we claim it for, and in the name of our Lord and

God, Jehovah. Our opposition is not people; although it seems like we must go through people to get to the land.

When you are playing the game of chess, it seems like the enemy is the pawns, rooks, bishops, knights and other pieces on the board that are physically trying to take your pieces and subdue your king; but that is not the enemy in chess. In the game of chess, it would seem that your enemy is the person sitting across from you who is looking at you and talking to you during the game, but the person sitting in the chair across from you is not truly your enemy. Your enemy in the game of chess is the mind of the person sitting across from you; the mind that is devising the plan being operated through that person and carried out by the pieces on the board.

In this world, your enemy is not the people (pieces) you are in contact with that seem to be coming up against you. Your true enemy is not even the demons or unclean spirits that influence the actions of the people that you are up against. Your enemies are lucifer and his army of fallen angels that are dictating the battle being waged against you. Your enemies are the principalities, thrones, dominions, powers, rulers of the darkness of this age and spiritual hosts of wickedness in the heavenly places. These are the controlling entities that feed strategy and directions to the evil spirits and evil men on this earth that we are in contact with. While we do have to deal with flesh and blood, we do not fight against them because they are just pawns. While we deal with the evil and unclean spirits on this earth that influence, and sometimes control men and women, that is not our fight, because our Lord Jesus gave us authority over them. You do not fight against the things you have authority over; you command them. We fight against the strongmen; the fallen angels in varying levels of authority that control the kingdom of darkness.

Chapter Seventeen
The tactics

Now that we as anointed entrepreneurs and sons and daughters of the kingdom of God have defined who our enemy is, we need to know how he attacks us and fights us. When the company in the same industry as you are is trying to shut you down, how do you fight? Yes, you do the natural things that you must do to avoid being shut down, but your true battle is in the spirit realm. You must do battle in the spirit realm against these strongmen, and take authority over these evil spirits to effect the natural actions you are taking. That is how the battle is won.

So how is the spiritual battle fought? The Apostle Paul tells us what the battle is all about; what to be wary of and what to focus on.

> *"But those who desire to be rich fall into*
> *temptation and a snare, and into many foolish and*
> *harmful lusts which drown men in destruction*
> *and perdition. For the love of money is a root to all*
> *kinds of evil, for which some have strayed from the*
> *faith in their greediness and pierced themselves*
> *through with many sorrows. But you, O man of*
> *God, flee these things and pursue righteousness,*
> *godliness, faith, love, patience, gentleness. Fight*
> *the good fight of faith, lay hold on eternal life, to*
> *which you were also called and have confessed*
> *the food confession in the presence of many*
> *witnesses." (1 Timothy 6:9-12 NKJV)*

Oh, there is so much to be revealed in these four verses! The focus of the anointed entrepreneur is not to be rich; riches are the byproduct of wisdom; revelation from God which is carried out by faith. When an anointed entrepreneur gets caught up in seeking riches instead of God, the anointing is lost because the focus becomes natural and no longer has connection to the supernatural. When the anointed entrepreneur begins to desire the riches, they will always fall into temptation and a snare; the temptation is to side-tract the truth and compromise your integrity in God, in order to achieve a particular goal. This is a snare of the enemy.

When satan offered Jesus all the kingdoms of the world if Jesus would just bow down and worship him, that was a temptation.

Jesus knew the plan of God and what He must suffer to complete the will of God; so the temptation was for Jesus to get the desired and promised result, without going through the plan that God laid out, which included the suffering. This will always be one of the snares of the enemy; it is a trap designed to get you out of the will of God, and therefore into the will of the enemy. Once an anointed entrepreneur's focus leaves God and is drawn to riches, they are guaranteed to fall into many foolish and harmful lusts, which will drown them in destruction, perdition and ultimately lead to death; spiritual death and eventually physical death.

One of the statements that Paul makes, is often misquoted in more than one way.

> *"The love of money is a root to all kinds of evil,*
> *for which some have strayed from the faith."*
> *(1Timothy 6:10 NKJV)*

Ultimately, Paul is saying that the desire of money over the desire of the plan of God is one of the roots to all different kinds of evil; from stealing to lying, cheating, sexual sins, murders and other kinds of sins. The goal of the enemy is to get you out of faith,

> *"...for whatever is not of faith is sin."*
> *(Romans 14:23 NKJV)*

It is through greediness that the anointed entrepreneur pierce themselves through with may sorrows. It is not the devil that pierces them; they do it to themselves by exchanging the truth of God for the lie.

Paul tells us what the fight is about; *"fight the good fight of faith"*. *(1 Timothy 6:12 NKJV)*. The fight is about your faith; the just or 'those who are justified by God', live and walk by faith. That is the difference between the walk of the sons of the kingdom of darkness and the sons of the kingdom of light; the sons of the kingdom of light walk by faith in God. Faith in God is faith in His

Word about His Son Jesus. The fight that the anointed entrepreneur, and the entire body of Christ is in, is a fight to abide in the Word and let His Word abide in us.

How do we fight the good fight of faith? By pursing righteousness, godliness, faith, love, patience, gentleness. We fight the good fight of faith by abiding in the Word and love of Jesus, so we may lay hold on eternal life. We fight the good fight of faith by being "strong in the Lord and in the power of His might" (Ephesians 6:10 NKJV), which means; knowing the Word of God and operating in that Word.

> *"If you abide in My Word, you are My disciples*
> *indeed. And you shall know the truth, and the*
> *truth shall make you free." (John 8:31,32 NKJV).*

Chapter Eighteen
The weapons of war and their purpose

Anointed entrepreneur, you must use your weapons to wage war in the earth, so that you can dispossess the land in order to possess it. In order to wage war against the enemies of your faith, you must be well acquainted with the weapons of your warfare; what they are, what are they for and how to use them.

First, let's talk about what your weapons are for, so we can get a good understanding of what they will do. Scripture says;

> "For though we walk in the flesh, we do not war according to the flesh. For the weapons of our warfare are not carnal but mighty in God for the pulling down of strongholds, casting down arguments and every high thing that exalts itself against the knowledge of God, bringing every thought into captivity to the obedience of Christ, and being ready to punish all disobedience when your obedience is fulfilled."
> (2 Corinthians 10:3-6 NKJV)

Okay, let's unpack the previous verse. We live in a physical body and in a physical world, but we do not war (we do not try to obtain the purposes of God) according to the flesh (the rules of the physical world). We do not war according to the flesh, because we are new creations in Christ, and have been given all of the weapons we need, in order to possess the promises of God. However, our weapons are not fleshly nor physical weapons, since our fight is not a fleshly or physical fight. We have said that our war is a spiritual war, being fought by spiritual beings. Their plan on how to defeat us is to disable our faith in God and in the operation of His Word in our lives.

How does the enemy try to disable our faith? The enemy tries to disable our faith by creating strongholds in our minds. The true battleground where the war for our faith happens in our minds.

A stronghold is defined as; *'a place where a particular cause or belief is strongly defended or upheld.'* For example, let's say you believe the scripture when it says,

"He was wounded for our transgression, He was bruised for our iniquities; the chastisement for our peace was upon Him, and by His stripes we are healed." (Isaiah 53:5 NKJV)

You believe this verse, but all of a sudden, a virus comes upon you and you can't seem to shake it. What happens is; the thoughts start to come into your mind that this sickness is not going to leave- it is here to stay. In your mind, every day you see or feel the symptoms of this sickness, you believe it a little more. You know what the scripture says, but the sickness seems to be staying in place day after day. You may be coughing or you may have chills, or any other symptom that seems to back up the idea that you are sick. Soon, the thought that you are sick begins to take hold, not the Word that you are healed; all because you have the physical, natural symptoms of a sickness.

Once the thought that you are sick begins to lodge in your mind, it becomes a stronghold; a particular belief that is strongly defended and upheld. The belief that you are sick is defended, because you are showing in your body the symptoms and signs of a person who is sick; it is being upheld because your mind says that if you are showing the symptoms and signs of a person who is sick, then you must be sick. After all, if it looks like a duck, walks like a duck and quacks like a duck, then it must be a duck, right?

However, the Word of God says that you are healed, no matter what the symptoms say. The question is; how do you appropriate the healing that the scripture says, instead of living the word that the stronghold says? This is the fight of faith. The weapons of our warfare were given to us so we could destroy the strongholds, like the one we are examining now. The way we use our weapons to pull down this stronghold is by "casting down arguments and every high thing that exalts itself against the knowledge of God, bringing every thought into captivity to the obedience of Christ" We go back to the Word of God and the faith that we walk and live by. The Word of God says that the stripes that Jesus took in

His flesh, healed us from all our diseases and sicknesses. We speak that Word; every time you cough or feel achy or throw up, you speak that Word. You may have gone to the doctor and maybe they gave you an antibiotic; every time you take that antibiotic, you quote the Word of God. No matter what your mind tells you or how your body feels, you live in the present Word that God has spoken, by speaking the same thing with confidence that the Word of God is true and established. That is how we establish on earth the Word that God has spoken and established in Heaven.

We cannot allow the stronghold in our mind that says 'if it looks like a duck, walks like a duck and quacks like a duck then it must be a duck" to take root and remain. No, there are no ducks in our minds, so we do not care what it looks like, walks like or sounds like. If we abide in Jesus, then we know the truth (by His stripes we are healed), and the truth that we know will set us free. The truth is that we use the power of God, which is resident in His Word to pull down the stronghold by casting down arguments (every thought that comes to your mind giving you a reason to believe that the physical symptoms are relaying a spiritual truth). We use the Word of God to cast down every high thing that exalts itself against the knowledge of God; every thought, doctor, google search, relative, etc., that is operating in opposition to what God has said about you in Christ. We bring every single thought into captivity to the obedience of Christ. Every single time the thought comes to your mind that you must be sick, you immediately combat it by repeating what the Word of God says, that by His stripes you are healed. It doesn't matter how long it takes to appropriate your healing. If your healing is not manifested immediately, do not worry and do not stop living and speaking the Word of God. You are in a war, and we know that not all wars end quickly.

Continue to fight the good fight of faith until you have the victory you are expecting. You obtain the victory in the Word of God, and you do it by pulling down strongholds; casting down every thought, every imagination, every argument and every high thing that exalts itself against the knowledge of God- which is the knowledge of His Word in Christ Jesus. You bring every single thought into captivity to the obedience of Christ; every single moment of every single day, until the victory is yours in the natural. You may have hundreds or thousands of thoughts every day that is contrary to what the Word of God says; and you must bring every one of those thoughts into captivity to the obedience of Christ. This is why the war is constant; just as your thoughts never stop, the war for your faith never stops.

Chapter Nineteen
What are your weapons?

We have discussed how to use your weapons to pull down the strongholds, but what exactly are the weapons that we use in order to pull down these strongholds, cast down these arguments and every high thing that exalts itself against the knowledge of God, and bring every thought into captivity to the obedience of Christ? Perhaps, if we can pinpoint exactly what the weapons of our warfare are that are so mighty in God to do all of the aforementioned things, we can live victorious in our lives and see constant and consistent victory as anointed entrepreneurs.

The weapons of our spiritual warfare are laid out for us in the book of Ephesians. Right after we find out what our spiritual armor is that keeps us safe from the hits and darts we take from the enemy, we are told what our weapons are that we use to fight back;

> *"And take the helmet of salvation, and the sword of the Spirit, which is the Word of God; praying always with all prayer and supplication in the Spirit, being watchful to this end with all perseverance and supplication for all the saints."*
> *(Ephesians 6:17,18 NKJV)*

Now we are getting to it! The offensive weapons of our warfare are the Sword of the Spirit, which is the Word of God, and praying always with all prayer and supplication in the Spirit. Our weapons are (1) the Word of God, (2) praying with all prayer, (3) and supplication in the spirit. The Word of God speaks for itself; we fight as we live, by every Word that comes out of the mouth of God. That means we fight and live by the written Word (Logos), the Word spoken to our spirit by the Holy Spirit (Rhema), and by the Word given to us by God's prophets (revealed).

The weapons of our warfare also consist of all prayer, meaning all types of prayer that we find revealed in the written Word of God. The prayer of faith, agreement, thanksgiving, Worship, petition, consecration, intercession, imprecation, praise, binding and loosing, warfare...all of these are weapons against the enemy.

We also have for a weapon supplication in the spirit; we can go to God in our Spirit language and let the Holy Spirit pray through us and for us, the perfect will of God.

We are also told to use these weapons to be consistently watchful, not just for ourselves but also for all of the saints; which means that if we as sons and daughters of the Most High are obedient to the Word of God, there should never be a time that any saint anywhere in the world does not have someone praying for them and interceding for their victory. If we are praying in the Spirit, the Holy Spirit can pray the perfect will of God for anyone, anywhere, to help them overcome.

How built up will you be, knowing that in addition to your prayers going up before God, that the entire body of Christ that is obedient to the Word of God is praying for your victory as well? Now thinking of that sickness that was trying to manifest in your body through the signs of 'symptoms', if you are using the weapons of your warfare, can you see how the strongholds are thrown down? Can you see how the imaginations, and every high thing and every thought that tries to exalt itself against the truth of God's Word is destroyed? Can you see how you and your business win?

Don't forget, not only do you, as the anointed entrepreneur, overcome every enemy and win every battle when you are fighting them according to the Word, but if you are watchful you will begin to see the battles before they arrive, through the Spirit of God;

> "However, when He, the Spirit of Truth, has come,
> He will guide you into all truth; for He will not speak
> on His own authority, but whatever He hears He will
> speak; and He will tell you things to come."
> (John 16:13 NKJV)

So, tell me anointed entrepreneur; if you abide in His Word and His Word abides in you, how can you possibly lose? How can your business possibly fail?

Chapter Twenty
The Strong Man

Before we begin to talk about this topic, let's get a definition of what a strongman is, so we are on the same page. The definition to be used in this section as our agreed upon understanding of a strongman is; *"a leader who rules by the exercise of threats, force or violence."* Merriam-Webster's dictionary also defines a strongman as; *"one who leads or controls by force of will and character or by military methods."*

Have no doubt about it; as sons and daughters of the kingdom of God and as anointed entrepreneurs, we are in a war. Our leader is Jesus Christ; not only has He already defeated our foe, but He has also sent the Spirit of God to be with us and aid us in maintaining the victory He has won, and to take more ground for His kingdom. The new ground that we take for the kingdom of God are; souls won for the kingdom and land possessed for the kingdom. We are to penetrate the land behind the gates of hell by kicking them down and possessing the land in the Name of Jesus.

So, who is the strongman and why should we be concerned with him? In the book of Matthew (as well as Mark), an interesting story is recorded that specifically relates to the strongman.

There was a particular person brought to Jesus who was demon possessed; which caused him to also be blind and mute. Everyone knew this person because this man's issues are clearly recorded. In addition, the reaction to this possessed, blind and mute man's deliverance was so radical that it actually changed and solidified minds about who Jesus was.

Jesus' restoration of this demon possessed man was so thorough, not only did the demon vacate the man, but the man could now see and speak as well. The people who were surrounding Jesus and witnessed this deliverance and restoration were so amazed that they said, *"could this be the Son of David?"* It is important to note that this particular deliverance was so amazing and so radical that the people began to view Jesus as the Messiah that they had been waiting for; they contemplated Him by His Messianic title given in the Scriptures. This is huge, because the minds of the masses were beginning to understand revelation from God Himself about Jesus. In their minds Jesus was becoming a different revelation to them. He was no longer just a prophet or just a righteous man, He was beginning to seem like the Son of the Most High God in their midst, just like the Scriptures had promised.

Immediately after this revelation of Jesus; as Christ began to fill the minds and hearts of the people, satan had to immediately come and put a stop to this revelation. How did satan do it? By speaking through his devoted earthly generals to sway the minds of the people back from the light of God's revelation, to ignorance of godly things through darkness. This is why some of the fallen angels are titled *"rulers of the darkness of this age"*; their goal is to keep people in such darkness that the light of God's Word and revelation cannot penetrate their minds. It is the god of this world that keeps the blindfold on the eyes of the children of this world; so that they will remain in darkness and not see the light of God's truth about who Jesus Christ is.

The pharisees heard the people begin to consider whether Jesus could truly be the Son of David, and immediately began to say that Jesus was in league with Beelzebub, ruler of the demons. By saying Jesus was doing these amazing things through the power of Beelzebub, they were denying the Lordship of Jesus, and trying to make the people recant their thoughts and words about who Jesus was. If the pharisees could convince the people that Jesus is in league with the ruler of demons, they could effectively reverse the belief about who Jesus was, and make them question the purpose of all of the miracles that Jesus had done, was doing and would do. If Jesus is in agreement with the lord of the demons, then not only should they not believe what Jesus says, but they should run from Jesus and consider Him an enemy. What person who is truly searching for God wants to be in league with demons?

On a side note, we see through this exchange what blasphemy against the Holy Spirit is. Blasphemy against the Holy Spirit, a sin that Jesus says during this exchange that will not be forgiven, is 'willfully and purposefully attributing the Work done by the Spirit of God to the devil in order to sway the minds of the masses and become God in His place." Where do we get this definition for blasphemy against the Holy Spirit? When Jesus cast out the demon from this possessed man and healed him, whom they all knew was demon possessed, blind and dumb, the people started to believe that Jesus was the Son of David- the coming King of Israel whom God said that He would send to them. This realization and revelation from God were strong enough to not only change the minds about who Jesus is, but it would also change the very nation of Israel itself from that moment on. In an attempt to keep the children of Israel in darkness and dissuade them about the true identity and nature of who Jesus was, and for the purpose of keeping the people submitted to them as their spiritual authority, the pharisees tried to willfully deceive the people. The pharisees were saying that the power that Jesus was using to do this deliverance, was the power of a strongman; Beelzebub, the lord of the demons. If the pharisees could get the people to believe what they were saying about Jesus, and where He obtained His supernatural power, they could retain their power and spiritual authority over the people. The pharisees purposefully attributed the power of God given by the Holy Spirit, whom they knew was from God, as demonic; and they purposely tried to convince other people that the work they knew was from God was in fact from the devil himself. That is blasphemy against the Holy Spirit as explained by Jesus in Matthew 12:25-32.

Back to the strongman. In the exchange between Jesus and the pharisees that we are currently discussing, Jesus says;

*"But if I cast out demons by the Spirit of God,
surely the kingdom of God has come upon you.*

*Or how can one enter a strong man's house and
plunder his goods, unless he first binds the
strong man? And then he will plunder his house."
(Mathew 12:28,29 NKJV)*

Jesus tells the pharisees (although He is really explaining this to
the people), that in order for one to change the effects that the
kingdom of darkness has over the physical world and its
inhabitants, that person must be operating by the Spirit of God.
Jesus confirmed that the kingdom of darkness was indeed a
kingdom; and as such, this kingdom had rulers and workers. Jesus
also confirms through this exchange that there is a lord over
demons, and that lord is considered a strongman. Jesus explains
that since a kingdom divided against itself cannot stand, He had to
be binding the strongman and casting out the demon by the
power of God. Jesus is showing in power that the kingdom of
satan was being overtaken by something ever more powerful; the
kingdom of God.

Here is the principle in all of this that Jesus is trying to get humans
to understand; you cannot overcome the kingdom of darkness
unless you bind the strongman. You have to bind the strongman
in order to take what is in his possession.

As an anointed entrepreneur, you must bind the strongman over
the house (or area) you are trying to possess, in order to possess
it. For example, if you are trying to open up a profitable store in
an area controlled by a strongman of thievery, you have to bind
that strongman to go into that area, effect change, and be
consistently successful. If you are opening a non-profit
organization to prevent suicide in an area with a high suicide rate,
you have to bind the strongman of death and destruction that is
over that area. If you want to sell your goods around the world on
the internet, you have to bind the strongman over the internet,
perhaps the prince of the power of the air.

As an anointed entrepreneur you should be seeking God for the gift of discerning of spirits to find out who is the strongman over the area that you are going in to possess; and once you find out, you go into battle in the spirit to bind that strongman so you can plunder his goods. Once you bind the strongman, you can cast out any and every demon operating in that area and take over, which is the action of dispossessing and possessing.

Now the question becomes, *'how do you bind a strongman once God gives you discernment of who that strongman is?'* We find the process back in Mathew 16:17-19;

> *"Jesus answered and said to him, 'Blessed are you, Simon Bar-Jonah, for flesh and blood has not revealed this to you, but My Father who is in heaven. And I say to you that you are Peter, and on this rock I will build My church, and the gated of Hades shall not prevail against it. And I will give to you the keys to the kingdom of heaven, and whatever you bind on earth shall be bound in heaven, and whatever you loose on earth shall be loosed in heaven." (NKJV)*

It is important that we unpack this scripture, because the process is in it. First, we seek God. In return for seeking God, He will reveal to us His Son Jesus- who Jesus is, in relation to what we are seeking God about. God has designed to make Himself known in Jesus; so anything we need or need to know, comes through our knowledge of who Jesus is. If we need healing, God reveals Jesus to us as the healer. If we need deliverance, God reveals Jesus to us as the deliverer. If we need wisdom, God reveals Jesus to us as the wisdom of the Father. Jesus is everything; He is the glory of God. Jesus is the direct expression of God; He is the Word of God, He is God in every facet that we need.

Once the Father reveals Jesus to us, Jesus immediately reveals to us who we are in Him. Jesus tells us that we are the righteousness of God in Him. Jesus tells us that we are ambassadors of the gospel in His name. Jesus tells us we are the salt of the earth, the light of God and city set on a hill that cannot be hid. Jesus tells us that we are His disciples and His friends; with the power to heal the sick, cast out demons, walk on serpents and scorpions without being harmed...in Him. Jesus tells us that we are His authority in the earth, that has his authority and power to effect change on this earth in His name, for God's glory. This is the rock that Jesus said He will build His church on, revelation from God about who Jesus is and then revelation from Jesus about who we are in Him.

Once you have revelation from both God and Jesus, you cannot help but operate in the faith of God and the power of the Spirit of God. This is why the gates of hades cannot prevail against you. No gate of hades can stop you from kicking it down and possessing the land inside the gates. No man will be able to stand before you all the days of your life, and no demon will be able to stay once you cast it out in Jesus Name.

Furthermore, Jesus has given us the keys to the kingdom of heaven. What are the keys of the kingdom of heaven? The keys of the kingdom of heaven are individual revelations from God about Jesus and from Jesus about you that allows you to overcome any obstacle, kick through any gate, and possess any bit of land that is held by the kingdom of darkness. Greater is He that is in you than he that is in the world. In addition, Jesus tells us once we have revelation from God through Him, we have the power to use that revelation to do war; to bind and loose on earth.

As mentioned in the previous chapter, the original translation of this verse on binding and loosing should be translated as;

> *"And I will give you the keys to the kingdom of heaven, and whatever you bind on earth shall be, having been bound in heaven, and whatsoever you loose on earth shall be, having been loosed in heaven."*

What God is saying is that with revelation from on High, we defeat the kingdom of darkness by first binding and loosing on earth what has been bound and loosed in heaven. We must bind the strongman in the name of Jesus on earth because he is bound in heaven. God's Word and will is established in heaven, but we must establish it here on earth. There is no sickness in heaven; sickness is bound in heaven and it is our job to bind it on earth. There is no lack in heaven, so it is our job to bind lack and loose the provision of God here on earth. This goes for everything; if it does not exist or operate in heaven, then it should not exist or operate in the kingdom of heaven on earth. Jesus has given us the power to bind and loose on earth what is bound and loosed in heaven, because we sit in heavenly places in Christ Jesus.

The Gem; whoever has an ear to hear, let them hear
What this looks like on earth is this; if God has given you an assignment as an anointed entrepreneur and you are in war against the strongman of a particular field or industry, you are to seek God for His purposes and for discerning of spirits in that area. The Spirit of God will reveal Jesus to you as the author and finisher of your faith, and Jesus will reveal who you are in Him. The Holy Spirit will then take over by teaching you what you do not know (wisdom), and telling you what He has heard from the throne room. The Holy Spirit declares to you all of the wisdom and provisions that Jesus has for you, so you can complete the assignment He has given you. Jesus gives you the power to do whatever needs to be done to get His Word (command) accomplished. You bind the strongman spirits that are controlling the things in the world that pertain to your assignment through your prayers, and by faith in the Word of God. In faith, you take the revelation, information and power you receive from Jesus through the Holy Spirit, and declare on earth what God has said in the heavens. You then go about doing the Word of the Lord; casting down every thought, imagination and high thing that attempts to exalt itself against the knowledge of Jesus and tries to speak a word contrary to what Jesus has spoken to you. You cast out every demon that presents itself along your path, and kick

down every gate of hell that is erected and trying to keep you out. Finally, you rebuke every unseen force that kicks up a storm, and speak to every visible thing that is affected by that unseen force and say to it, "Peace. Be still."

This is how you war according to the Spirit, to dispossess the enemy and possess the land that God has already given you. Once you achieve the goal, you go back to the Father to find out the next strategy or assignment.

Before we end this chapter, I want to share something that the Holy Spirit opened up to me recently. I was reading John chapter 15, where Jesus is talking about Himself being the vine, our Father being the vinedresser and us being the branches that are supposed to be bearing fruit. I got to verses 7 and 8 and the Spirit showed me something I found amazing;

> *"If you abide in Me, and My Words abide in you,*
> *you will ask what you desire, and it shall be done*
> *for you. By this My Father is glorified, that you*
> *bear much fruit, so you will be My disciples."*
> *(NKJV)*

What I was shown is this; Jesus tells us that just as the Father sent Him, He has sent us. That means what we have seen of Jesus was the Father sending Him and Jesus obeying the Father. Jesus was abiding in the Father and the Father's Words were abiding in Him. If Jesus was abiding in the Father and the Father's Words were abiding in Him, then He must have asked what He desired and it was done for Him; and by what was done for Him, the Father was glorified and Jesus bore much fruit. We know that God was glorified in Jesus, and that Jesus bore much fruit.

My question became, 'well if Jesus was abiding in the Father, the Father's Words were abiding in Jesus, and because of that Jesus could ask what He will and it was done for Him...what did Jesus ask the Father for?' Jesus must have asked the Father for something daily because He was abiding in the Father and the

Father's Word was abiding in Him. The Holy Spirit said, "well, the answer to that question is the fruit: if God was glorified in Jesus, and Jesus bore much fruit, what fruit did Jesus bear?"

If I identify the fruit I see in Jesus' life, then I can find out what Jesus was asking the Father for, right? I identified that Jesus was asking the Father daily, to destroy the works of the devil. I identified that Jesus was asking for God to set the captives free. In other words, God had revealed to Jesus his assignment and Jesus was asking for the assignment that God had revealed to Him to be fulfilled every day of His life. Jesus wanted the anointing on Him to be realized in the earth...so what was that anointing that was on Jesus?

> "The Spirit of the Lord is upon Me, because He
> has anointed Me to preach the gospel to the poor;
> He has sent me to heal the brokenhearted, to
> proclaim liberty to the captives, and recovery of
> sight to the blind, to set at liberty those who are
> oppressed; to proclaim the acceptable year of
> the Lord." (Luke 4:18,19 NKJV)

Jesus was able to affect the kingdom of darkness because He was walking in the revealed assignment of God for Him, which allowed the anointing of God- the Spirit of God -to work the works of God in His life so that God would be glorified. When Jesus went off to Himself to pray, He prayed for the anointing that He had been given to operate; the gospel preached to the poor, the healing of the brokenhearted, the proclamation of liberty to the captives, the recovery of sight to the blind, liberty for those who were oppressed of the devil. We saw the fruit of this prayer in the ministry of Jesus.

So what is your assignment? If you are an anointed entrepreneur, what ministry has God given you so that He can be glorified? If God is not glorified in your business, how can it be anointed of God? If there is no fruit that glorifies God, how can you say that the Spirit of the Lord is upon you to do it? And if the Spirit of the Lord is not upon you to do it, how will you war against the enemy? God tells us in His Word that it is His anointing that breaks the yoke;

> "The Lord of hosts has sworn saying, 'Surely, as I
> have thought, so it shall come to pass, and as
> I have purposed, so it shall stand: That I will
> break the Assyrian in My land, and on My
> mountains tread him underfoot. Then his yoke
> shall be removed from them, and his burden
> removed from their shoulders.' This is the purpose
> that is purposed against the whole earth, and
> this is the hand that is stretched out over all the
> nations. For the Lord of hosts has purposed, and
> who will annul it? His hand is stretched out, and
> who will turn it back?" (Isaiah 14:24-27 NKJV)

How will the Assyrian be broken in His Land? How will the yoke be removed? Let's go back to the Scripture and seek out answer;

> "It shall come to pass in that day that his burden
> will be taken away from your shoulder, and his yoke
> from your neck, and the yoke will be destroyed
> because of the anointing oil." (Isaiah 10:27 NKJV)

The yoke is broken by the anointing of God, the Holy Spirit. This is why is it so important to seek God for revelation; because revelation will point you to Jesus, who will tell you who you are and what your assignment is. Then the Holy Spirit can teach you all things and give you the power you need to effect change in the earth for the kingdom of God. If you have your assignment, then fight the good fight of faith and lay hold to the promise.

Chapter Twenty-one
Faith and the promise

As an anointed entrepreneur, and especially as a son and daughter of the kingdom of God, we should have a battle-ready attitude when it comes to anything that tries to shake our faith. We already know that the gates of hell are trying to prevail to keep us out of the land so we will not take it over. We already know that we are in a fight for our faith with the enemy of our faith and with the fallen angels that have rulership over certain aspects in the spiritual realm. When it comes to the things and systems of this world, these spirits have influence over the sons of disobedience, to the point that these sons of disobedience can even be possessed by demonic and unclean spirits on this earth. The fight for our faith is a fight for our lives, because the just live by faith.

However, we also know that we overcome the world by the Blood of the Lamb and the word of our testimony. We have authority in Jesus' Name to bind and loose; we can bind the strongmen and rulers of the darkness of this world and in high places, as well as every other power that is not of our God. We know that we have been given power and authority to cast out demons and unclean spirits; greater is He that is in us than he that is in the world. We win; we are more than conquerors and our position in this earth should be to glorify God by completing the work He has given us to do, destroying the works of darkness all along the way.

Our Father has given us every single thing that pertains to life and godliness; He is not going to give it to us, He has already given it to us. We have the Spirit of the living God residing in us, what can we not do, in Jesus' Name? What will our God not give us, since He has sent His Word, His only begotten Son to die a horrible death (the death that each one of us deserved to die), on our behalf? Who is the one who dares stand before us to condemn us to anything that is not God's thoughts towards us?

Yet they will try; the world will try to keep us down, and make us believe that we have no claim to anything in this world, and that we will lose every battle. The enemy will try to make us afraid; as he roars like a lion in the economic system, the educational system, the political system, the policing system, the religious system, the financial system, the entertainment system and every other system of this world that satan has control over. Yet our God says that He has gone before us and fought the battle for us, and that He is with us and will never leave us nor forsake us. Our God tells us;

> "No man shall be able to stand before you all the days of your life, as I was with Moses, so I will be with you. I will not leave you nor forsake you. Be strong and of good courage, for to the people you shall divide as an inheritance the land which I swore to their fathers to give them. Only be strong and very courageous, that you may observe to do according to all the law which Moses My servant commanded you, do not turn from it to the right hand or to the left that you may prosper wherever you go. This Book of the Law shall not depart from your mouth, but you shall meditate in it day and night, that you may observe to do according to all that is written in it. For then you will make your way prosperous, and then you will have good success. Have I not commanded you? Be strong and of good courage; do not be afraid, nor be dismayed, for the Lord your God is with you wherever you go." (Deuteronomy 1:5-9 NKJV)

This is an awesome Word. We must appropriate this Word for ourselves today because this is an everlasting Word. We are the heirs of the promise through Abraham because we have believed God's Word about Jesus the Christ. To appropriate this Word to ourselves, we must replace Moses' name with the Name of Jesus;

> *"...as I was with Jesus, so I will be with you."*

and,

> *"Only be strong and very courageous, that you may observe to do according to all the law which Jesus My servant commanded you..."*

Next, we appropriate this Scripture by replacing *"the Law"* with *"the Word"*, because we are not under the law, we are under Grace. Jesus came to fulfill the Law, and to give us the Word (Himself). Finally, we need to be specific in our obedience to this Word; we have to be strong and courageous in order to observe to do (make sure we understand it and do it) according to all the Word which Jesus commanded us. We are not to turn from the Word Jesus commanded us to the right hand nor the left. This means that we are not to change the Word, short-change the Word nor try to find a way to circumvent the Word (get around straight obedience to it), and then we will make our way prosperous and then we will have good success. Be strong to do all of the Word and be of good courage that you are doing the right thing when you choose strict adherence to the Word over the world's way of operating. Do not be afraid to speak up for what is right in God's sight and do not be dismayed when it seems like you are taking a loss because you are doing business the way God intended. Why? Because the Lord your God is with you wherever you go.

As an anointed entrepreneur, there will be times when a seeming opportunity will come your way and you know that if you just bend a little, it could cause big things to happen for you.

Perfect example

I have a great product I invented and My Father told me is going to be very successful. A year and a half after I had the product manufactured, after a lot of back and forth, I submitted my product to be on the Shark Tank television show. I knew if I could just walk on that stage and show my product, I would make millions.

When I submitted my idea to casting, I was contacted right away, because they loved my product and were creating a path for me to be on the show. However, I quickly found out that during the process of getting on the show I would have to lie, I would have to tell a deliberate lie and misrepresent myself to secure my spot on the show. What do I do? I know that God gave me the idea and caused me to be able to manufacture that idea because He created an extraordinary path for me to get it done.

Once I came up with the idea for the product and did the work of faith by designing the product in all aspects, knowing while I was designing it that I didn't have the tens of thousands of dollars it would take to manufacture the product and bring it to market, God created a way for me to get the money by bringing a unique group of investors across my path, who basically gave me the money to do it for the smallest amount of return on their investment.

I had the game manufactured and started selling it online, but the sales were not as big as I knew they should be. It was selling, but not in the big numbers I wanted them to sell. I struggled with applying for Shark Tank, because to me that would be abandoning my faith that God could make me successful if I kept faith in His Word. I felt this way because going to Shark Tank seemed to me like I was going to man to seek their approval, money and influence to get something out that God clearly blessed me with. I am not saying anything about how you do your business, and I am not saying that it is a sin to go on Shark Tank. I am just talking about how I felt in this particular instance; I believed that since God had made the provision for me to come up with the idea and gave me a path to getting almost thirty thousand dollars to manufacture the product, He was more than able to provide the sales of the product.

After continually listening to people tell me that I should go on Shark Tank, and wanting to get some sales and acknowledgement for an incredibly innovative product that I had created, I applied to Shark Tank and now they had contacted me to complete the application process for the show. The only problem is that I would have to misrepresent myself in a particular area to make it through the application.

So now I am faced with this choice; I can tell a big lie and wiggle my way onto the show (hoping they don't catch me in the lie), and get hundreds of thousands of dollars from man's provision. I could go through the process of partnering with unsaved men and make millions of dollars right away, or I could trust God by not lying and wait on Him and His plan for that level of prosperity in my life. What would you do when faced with these choices? Would you tell the lie, get the money and repent later, or would you stay true to the Word of God to you from the beginning?

A lot of people would forsake the anointing and go for the money. A lot of entrepreneurs will stay entrepreneurs but lose the anointing, because they would rather have the end result quickly without having to completely trust God.

Jesus was faced with this same dilemma when satan came to Him and offered Him all of the glory of the kingdoms of this world (systems, industries, wealth, fame...everything a man could desire), if He would just take the shortcut and bow down to lucifer instead of doing it God's way and going through the process and through His cross.

What will you do when offered a shortcut to the glory that God has already promised you through your business? As for me, I turned it down. I decided to withdraw from the application process. Does it haunt me? No. I will admit that from time to time, it comes to mind and for a few seconds I chastise myself by saying, 'I could have been super rich right now'. However, I cast down those vain imaginations with the Word of God. I remind myself that observing to do what I know is truth, and waiting on God to bring me into the place that He has for me is so much more important because,

> *"The blessing of the Lord makes on rich, and He adds no sorrow with it." (Proverbs 10:22)*

I don't know what the results of making a deal with those men, based on a lie, would have been. I don't know if they would have found out and embarrassed me on national television by calling me a liar and devious businessman. I don't know what sorrow would come with choosing the short-cut over the process. I don't know if I would have been treated fairly (after all, the super-rich don't all become super-rich because they play by the rules), and I don't know what else I would have felt like I had to sacrifice in order to obtain or to keep that wealth. I do believe that I would have lost the anointing in going that way; and what good is a business in this life if it is not anointed? If it is not anointed, God is not in it and if God is not in it, why should I as a son of God be in it?

I am happy for whatever the outcome will be, and thrilled that I can stand before my Lord every single morning and pray that I receive this day my daily bread; knowing that I will receive it and that He will lead me and guide me this day into all of His will. I will trust in the Lord for my life and for my business that He has given me, and in return, He promises to never leave me nor forsake me. My God has promised to make my name great and to give me the desires of my heart. What more can I ask for? I am so very grateful.

Where do you stand; are you an entrepreneur or are you an anointed entrepreneur? There is a difference. The entrepreneur walks as a wise one, learning from experience and standing on what they know or can learn through experience. The anointed entrepreneur stands in faith, learning from revelation and wisdom given to them by the living God. The anointed entrepreneur has a promise; that if they acknowledge God in all of their ways, He will direct their paths. Would you rather have God directing your path or would your rather have man and worldly experience directing your path?

Faith. The anointed entrepreneur and every son and daughter of God walks by faith. What do you choose from this moment on? I say to you; choose faith, choose God.

Chapter Twenty-two
Good Success

Good success from God's perspective; what does that look like?

Good success from God's perspective looks like the completion of what He has called you to do. Before Jesus left this earth by way of the cross, He prayed;

> *"As you have given Him authority over all flesh,*
> *that He should give eternal life to as many as*
> *You have given Him. And this is eternal life, that*
> *they may know You, the only true God, and*
> *Jesus Christ whom You have sent. I have glorified*
> *You on the earth. I have finished the work You*
> *have given Me to do." (John 17:2-4 NKJV)*

and,

> *"I have manifested Your Name to the men whom*
> *You have given Me out of the world. They were*
> *Yours, You gave them to Me and they have kept*

Your Word. Now they have known that all things
which You have given Me are from You. For I
have given them the words which You have given
Me, and they have received them, and have known
surely that I came forth from You; and they have
believed that You have sent Me."
(John 17:6-8 NKJV)

Jesus had assignments from the Father while He was on this earth. Jesus was sent to the lost sheep of the tribe of Israel, to manifest the Name of Jehovah our Father to the men that the Father gave Him during His time on earth. The Father spoke in advance that not all would believe on Jesus as the manifestation of God Himself on the earth, but that as many as would believe, Jesus was to give them eternal life. Eternal life is to know God the Father and Jesus the Christ; not just to know of them but to experience a relationship with them through the regeneration and quickening of the spirit.

Jesus did these things; and that is why God was pleased with Him and accepted His life as a sacrifice for the sins of all of mankind. Jesus never displeased the Father through disobedience, a lack of faith, nor of any type of rebellion of His Word. Jesus walked in the perfect will of the Father, and that is why we can see supernatural fruits on Jesus' life everywhere He went. Jesus walked in power and authority; His Words never fell to the ground void and everything He spoke and did produced life- they became real- as in 'verifiable' and 'able to be witnessed.'

Jesus told us that as the Father sent Him, so He was sending us. That means that if we walk in the assignment that God has spoken over our lives, we can have the same effect on this earth that Jesus had. We can walk in the perfect will of the Father and we can see supernatural fruit on our lives everywhere we go. We can walk in power and authority; our words will never fall to the ground void and everything we speak will produce life- become real as in 'verifiable' and 'able to be witnessed'.

As an anointed entrepreneur and as a son and daughter of God, this is our lot; to reign in life through Christ. Reigning in life through Christ is good success and profitability. We often get things twisted because we think of profitability as monetary excess. We think this way because we are born into a natural world, and that is the imagery and language that has been spoken to us all of our lives on this earth. Every system of this world is geared towards making us equate success and value with money; the educational system, the economic system, the health care system...every single system you can think of is predicated on money. Even the religious system elevates money in the face of its parishioners. Every time we turn around, we hear something about money- why we should be getting it so that we can give it. Yes, the church does need money to operate and yes, we are mandated by God to give so that it can be given to us and so that there will be meat in His house for the work of the ministry to go throughout the earth. However, don't get it twisted; God said He would supply all of our needs according to His riches in glory, and money is not one of His riches in glory. God did not create money- man created money for the purpose of controlling other men. God's riches in glory is wisdom, love, forgiveness, mercy, grace, kindness, longsuffering and all of the things that He is and that Jesus displayed. Not once while Jesus walked this earth, not once did He say we had to give Him any money for Him to perform a miracle in the lives of the people, or for Him to cast out a demon from their lives. Not one time did Jesus preach a Word to the multitude and then say, "you can cash app me at $SonofMan" or "you need to sow a seed, I'm good ground". Jesus was the direct expression of the Father, and although He did allow people to give to His ministry (He had a person keeping the money bag, so there had to be money coming in), He never leaned on them and put a burden on the people to give. God said He is your provider; if you believe that, then do your assignment and leave the providing to God.

Am I discouraging giving to the work of God? Absolutely not; I practice giving and sowing in my life through tithes, offerings and seeds. I bring my tithes because I see it in the Word. I give my offering because I love my God and I want to give to Him of what He has given me; my money, my time and my life. I sow seeds because I want to bless people's lives since God has blessed me. I give to God because I love Him, not because someone has their elbow on my neck about it. If you are not giving out of love for God and love for people, as a result of the grace and mercy God has shown you, then you might as well keep your piece of change. God requires obedience, not sacrifice.

What we need to be seeking God for is wisdom; because wisdom is the principle thing. Yet, while we are seeking wisdom, we need to get some understanding. Wisdom will cause riches, wealth and honor to be in your house. Understanding will cause you to know God as a provider so that you will never horde money but you will be free with it as a resource that speaks in the earth. When you fall into a problem, such as not being able to pay your bills, don't go to God and ask for money; you go to God and ask for wisdom and favor. Wisdom will tell you what God has already provided for you to get through this moment and favor will cause you to not only get your bill paid, but to pay someone else's bill in addition to yours.

That is why we lack the things we need, because we are asking amiss. If we have understanding, we know that God is Jehovah Jireh, the Lord will provide. With understanding of who God is, we will know that we will never fall short in what we need. Never will the righteous be forsaken, nor will their seed beg bread. However, this Word is only manifested in your life if you know God, and you have faith in His Word. This Word will only be manifested in your life if you are obedient to the Word and do the things that are pleasing in His sight. Our God has told us;

> *"But without faith it is impossible to please Him, for*
> *he who comes to God must believe that He is, and*

that He is a rewarder of those who diligently seek Him." (Hebrews 11:6 NKJV)

Again, if you come to God for provision, you must first know that He is Jehovah Jireh and you must diligently seek Him as Jehovah Jireh, and have faith that He will provide what you need. If you are showing sickness in your body, you must go to God in faith knowing that He is Jehovah Rapha; the Lord God that sent His Word (Jesus) and healed you, and then you will receive the reward of your faith, which will be the healing that was provided. In order for the Word to work, you must do more than simply think it. The word used for believe is faith; you must know that He is. Know that He is what? Know that He is whatever you are in need of, through Jesus Christ. Remember that when we seek God, God reveals to us Jesus, because all of His provision to us come through Jesus Christ- because of His atoning work on the cross. On the cross at Calvary, Jesus signed the new testament between God and us with His blood. Therefore, all of the blessings that God has spoken in the old testament has been appropriated to us now, and none of the curses. That is why this covenant is better than the first; we have obtained the righteousness of God through Christ Jesus and all of the blessings come upon the righteous. There are no curses upon the righteous. Is that amazing or what!

As an anointed entrepreneur you have every single blessing of God that exists in the heavenlies! You cannot help but prosper in the natural, even as your soul prospers in God's Word. The more you seek God and know God, the more you understand who He is and who you are in Christ. God is with you and He will never leave you nor forsake you. God has already given you everything that pertains to life (natural) and godliness (spiritual). On top of all of this, He has given you His very Spirit; His Dunamis power. God has promised to go before you and fight for you. God has made a promise concerning you, if you abide in His Word and let His Word abide in you;

"he shall be like a tree planted by the rivers of

water, that brings forth its fruit in its season,
whose leaf also shall not wither and whatever
he does shall prosper." (Psalm 1:3 NKJV)

The blessings that God promises to you are too many to write here, without writing down just about the whole Bible. You are anointed and your God given business is your assignment; it is your ministry before Him. Seek first the kingdom of heaven and His righteousness and all the things that you need to conquer kingdoms and take over industries will be given to you. You will have the greatest business ever and God will bless you beyond measure. Our Father will bless you and make your name great and all of the families of the earth will be blessed by you, because He has given you the power to get wealth (not money, wealth- there is a distinct difference- although wealth generally includes lots and lots of money), so that He may establish His covenant which He swore.

Man of God, woman of God; you are anointed by the one true and living God; the Most High, the Lord of Hosts, the Almighty, the Everlasting God. Jehovah is His Name and He is everything you will ever need.

You are an anointed entrepreneur; given an assignment in the earth to be fruitful and multiply, subdue the earth and have dominion over it. You are called to subdue kingdoms and kick through the gates of hades and possess the land; everywhere the sole of your feet shall tread He has given it to you.

You are an anointed entrepreneur. Go forth in the name of the Lord Jesus Christ and let His will be done and His kingdom come on earth as it is in heaven.

In Jesus Name, go.